Raspberry Pi Retro Gaming

Build Consoles and Arcade Cabinets to Play Your Favorite Classic Games

Mark Frauenfelder

Ryan Bates

Apress®

Raspberry Pi Retro Gaming: Build Consoles and Arcade Cabinets to Play Your Favorite Classic Games

Mark Frauenfelder
Studio City, CA, USA

Ryan Bates
Pittsburgh, PA, USA

ISBN-13 (pbk): 978-1-4842-5152-2
https://doi.org/10.1007/978-1-4842-5153-9

ISBN-13 (electronic): 978-1-4842-5153-9

Managing Director, Apress Media LLC: Welmoed Spahr
Acquisitions Editor: Aaron Black
Development Editor: James Markham
Coordinating Editor: Jessica Vakili

Distributed to the book trade worldwide by Springer Science+Business Media New York, 233 Spring Street, 6th Floor, New York, NY 10013. Phone 1-800-SPRINGER, fax (201) 348-4505, e-mail orders-ny@springer-sbm.com, or visit www.springeronline.com. Apress Media, LLC is a California LLC and the sole member (owner) is Springer Science + Business Media Finance Inc (SSBM Finance Inc). SSBM Finance Inc is a **Delaware** corporation.

For information on translations, please e-mail rights@apress.com, or visit http://www.apress.com/rights-permissions.

Apress titles may be purchased in bulk for academic, corporate, or promotional use. eBook versions and licenses are also available for most titles. For more information, reference our Print and eBook Bulk Sales web page at http://www.apress.com/bulk-sales.

Any source code or other supplementary material referenced by the author in this book is available to readers on GitHub via the book's product page, located at www.apress.com/978-1-4842-5152-2. For more detailed information, please visit http://www.apress.com/source-code.

Printed on acid-free paper

Table of Contents

About the Authors

Mark Frauenfelder is a research director at Institute for the Future and the founder of Boing Boing, a web site about current events with five million monthly unique viewers. He was the founding editor-in-chief of *MAKE*, the only magazine exclusively devoted to do-it-yourself projects, and the founding editor-in-chief of *Wired* online. He was an editor at *Wired* magazine and *Wired* books from 1993 to 1998. He's also the editor-in-chief of Cool Tools, a tool review site with roots to the *Whole Earth Catalog*. Mark's also an artist and designer, and his work has appeared in group and solo gallery exhibitions throughout the United States. He designed Billy Idol's *Cyberpunk* CD cover, video box, and print advertisements. He lives in Los Angeles with his wife, writer Carla Sinclair (founding editor-in-chief of *CRAFT* magazine), and his two daughters.

Ryan Bates runs the arcade building web site RetroBuiltGames.com specializing in DIY kits and comprehensive tutorials for building mini arcades, claw machines, and other arcade/video game-related nostalgia. Ryan is a full-time fabrication instructor at the Carnegie Mellon Univeristy engineering makerspace in Pittsburgh, PA.

What's in This Book

The goal of *Raspberry Pi Retro Gaming* is to teach you how to set up a Raspberry Pi to play your favorite classic games and to show you how to make your own handheld, console, and bartop arcade cabinet using a Raspberry Pi. Here's a breakdown of the chapters:

Chapter 1: The World of Raspberry Pi Retro Gaming

Chapter goal: Introducing the world's current and most beloved single-board computer, the Raspberry Pi, and its reputation in the retro gaming community

Chapter 2: Setting Up the Raspberry Pi for Retro Gaming

Chapter goal: Getting familiar with the Raspberry Pi and emulators

Chapter 3: A Closer Look at RetroPie

Chapter goal: The things you'll need to know to use RetroPie to play different games, save games, and customize the interface

Chapter 4: Enclosure for Your Raspberry Pi

Chapter goal: a quick overview and comparison of readily available cases for the Raspberry Pi plus steps how to build your own

Chapter 5: Modern Fabrication Tools

Chapter goal: an introduction to modern tools and methods for cutting wood plus mechanical design fundamentals to start your first arcade cabinet build

Chapter 6: Installing the Electronics

Chapter goal: detail instructions covering the what and why regarding the electronic components of a miniature arcade cabinet

Chapter 7: Build a Desktop RetroPie Arcade

Chapter goal: Step-by-step instructions for building a larger bartop-sized arcade machine for two players on a budget

CHAPTER 1

The World of Raspberry Pi Retro Gaming

All the best games are easy to learn and difficult to master. They should reward the first quarter and the hundredth.

— Bushnell's Law

Gaming has its origins near the birth of computer technology, and like any first exposure to anything radically unconventional, it always leaves a lasting impression. We'll look back at the birth of video gaming, its genesis to mainstream culture, and the current renaissance of reliving the retro gaming era through emulation today.

Humble Beginnings

I spent most of the summer of 1983 fighting monsters in a multilevel dungeon. By day I was an engineer's assistant at a disk drive manufacturing plant in Boulder, Colorado. But the instant my workday was over, I'd jump in my car, make a pit stop at a fast-food place to buy a large bag of burgers or tacos, and then head straight to my friend Doug's house, where he and four other dungeon crawlers were huddled around Doug's brand-new Apple IIe.

© Mark Frauenfelder and Ryan Bates 2019
M. Frauenfelder and R. Bates, *Raspberry Pi Retro Gaming*,
https://doi.org/10.1007/978-1-4842-5153-9_1

They were waiting for me to enter the password for my character, a dwarf fighter named Phlegm, so we could start fighting bushwackers, bubbly slimes, wererats, giant spiders, undead kobolds, and other malevolent creatures that stood between us and treasure chests loaded with gold and loot.

The game was called Wizardry: Proving Grounds of the Mad Overlord (Figure 1-1). Released for the Apple II in 1981, the game pitted a party of up to six players against a menagerie of brutish monsters, spell-casting evil wizards, and other fiendish enemies that we encountered during our adventure through ten trap-filled levels of a complex maze-like dungeon, each of which was more harrowing than the level above it.

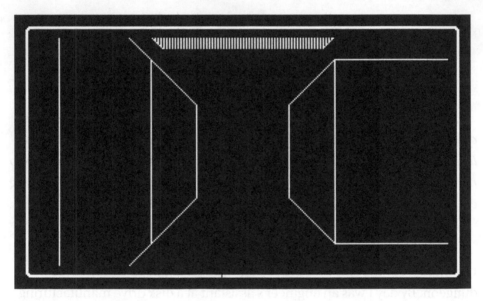

Figure 1-1. *Level one of the maze from Wizardry: Proving Grounds of the Mad Overlord*

Unlike today's dungeon crawlers that have built-in auto-mapping, *Proving Grounds of the Mad Overlord* required players to draw maps on sheets of graph paper. Woe to anyone who ventured into the dungeons without a map to guide them, for they would soon find themselves enveloped in blackness or hopelessly lost in a diabolical teleport trap. But for me, drawing a map and making up my own symbols to identify a trap door, a pit, a turntable, or a teleportal was part of the fun of playing the game. I felt like I was exploring an uncharted territory (see Figure 1-2).

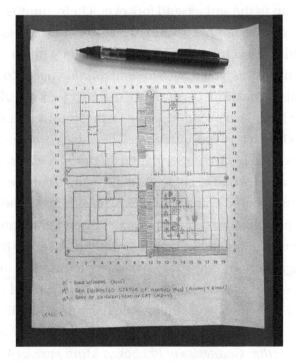

Figure 1-2. *Hand-drawn map from the first maze level of Wizardry: Proving Grounds of the Mad Overlord*

Proving Grounds of the Mad Overlord was a relentlessly unforgiving game. It automatically saved the state after every combat encounter, whether we wanted it to or not. And we often didn't want it to, especially when our characters were killed or had their levels drained by evil priests. And when a character died, it didn't automatically respawn at the surface, ready for another attempt. No, the corpse laid in the dungeon in the spot it had been killed. If your party happened to include a high-level priest, he or she could cast a resurrection spell to bring the dead adventurer back to life (it didn't always work); otherwise, surviving members had to drag the lifeless carcass up to the surface and fork over a hefty number of hard-won gold pieces at the Temple of Cant to resurrect the corpse. And if your entire party ended up getting killed in an encounter with an especially nasty group of monsters, you'd have to send *another* party down into the dungeon to collect the dead. It's no surprise that it took my friends and me all summer long—with sessions often lasting until 3:00 a.m.—to finally win the game. Our victory was bittersweet, because we no longer had a compelling reason to hang out. No matter, though. The fall semester was about to begin, and we had to get ready to go back to college.

I always remembered that summer I spent with my friends, drinking beer, looking up spells, and discussing tactics. After I graduated and moved to California, I bought my own copy of the *Wizardry* floppy disks and played it again on my newly purchased Apple IIe, enjoying the adventure as a solo player in charge of an entire party. I sold the computer around 1988, along with all my other Apple II games, including a bunch of Infocom text adventures that I loved playing: *Zork, Hitchhiker's Guide to the Galaxy, Leather Goddesses of Phobos, A Mind Forever Voyaging*, and the *Ultima* series of fantasy role-playing video games. By that time, I had a speedy Dell desktop machine with a 80386 processor and a whopping 640k of RAM, and I didn't think I'd ever be nostalgic about my IIe, with its 64k of RAM and no hard drive (how wrong I was).

Several decades later, when my younger daughter Jane became interested in adventure games, I thought it would be interesting to see if *Wizardry* would hold her interest. Maybe she could be my fellow adventurer, 35 years after the first time I played the game.

I poked around online and learned that *Proving Grounds of the Mad Overlord* was considered "abandonware"—the term used for software that was no longer for sale or supported by the publisher.[1] The software for the game was easily found online, as were emulators to run the DOS and Apple versions. I had a Raspberry Pi and discovered that there was an emulator called DOSBox that could run MS-DOS (Microsoft's first operating system) programs on the Pi. A few hours later, the title screen of *Proving Grounds of the Mad Overlord* appeared on the display attached to my tiny Pi. It had been over 30 years since I saw it. I felt like a time traveler.

I called Jane into my office and told her a bit about the game. I didn't know if she be interested, considering she was in the middle of playing *Zelda: Breath of the Wild*, an incredibly detailed, three-dimensional game, with fantastic music, challenging puzzles, side quests, and thrilling real-time battles with AI-powered monsters. How could the primitive, 1982 wireframe graphics and turn-based gameplay hold a candle to *Breath of the Wild*?

Fortunately, Jane was instantly enthralled by *Wizardry*. Creating new characters was basically like rolling dice to create a *Dungeons and Dragons* character, something she was already familiar with because we'd been in a father-daughter DnD club for a few years. She enjoyed taking the time to read the manual (which we found online as a PDF file), learning about the various races, classes, and spells. We each took ownership of three of the characters and entered the maze. Jane loved the fact that it was necessary to make a map of each level, and every time we had an encounter with a group of monsters, we discussed our options before engaging with the enemy. Our game progress was at the same pace as a regular DnD game, but that didn't bother us in the least. We were having a blast.

---

[1] Abandonware may still be under copyright. It's a good practice to check the copyright status before downloading abandonware.

WHY I LIKE RETRO-GAMES, BY JANE (AGE 15)

The first memory I have of playing a video game took place when I was just 4 or 5 years old. On our family computer, an old eMac, my sister would help me load up *Mickey's Kitchen*, a game where the player controls Mickey Mouse to create lots of different dishes for him and his friends to eat. I was completely infatuated with this game, as it had the power to transport me into a whole new universe in which I could bake anything I wanted (as a 4-year-old, I did not yet have that privilege). I continued playing video games as I grew up, as they all seemed to have this power of opening a door into a new world.

Then, in 6th grade, I got invited to my friend's birthday party at the Neon Retro Arcade, in Pasadena, California. The walls were lined with games like *Dig Dug* and *Donkey Kong*. Of course, I'd known about these games since elementary school. My favorite book was *Ready Player One*, and so I knew all about a few of them. But I had never seen them with my own eyes. I fell in love with many of the games (specifically *Q-Bert*, *Joust*, and *Robotron*) and I've now gone there several times, savoring the special occasion each time.

The simplicity of these games completely juxtapose the insane complexities of modern games and are able to put anyone into a state where time doesn't exist and the world around them fades. There aren't two billion rules to keep forgetting or other players to interact with. It's just you, the screen, and the goal. As simple as these games were, they were also new universes. The idea that such a simple game could have the same effect as the games that I grew up with was amazing. With so much less complexity than modern games, they could create the same outcome. From that point on, retro games have continued to fascinate me.

While Jane and I were playing, I started to wonder what other classic computer games were available to play via the DOSBox emulator. I soon discovered that there were *thousands* of games, including many that I loved playing in the 1980s and 1990s, including all the text adventures like *The Hitchhiker's Guide to the Galaxy (1985)*, *A Mind Forever Voyaging* (1985), *Amnesia* (1986), simulations like *SimCity* (1989) and *Railroad Tycoon* (1990), RPGs like *Ultima IV: Quest of the Avatar* (1985), strategy games like *Lemmings* (1991), action games like *Prince of Persia* (1990) and *Doom* (1993), and dungeon crawlers like *Rogue* (1983). I was soon hooked all over again on retro-games.

It turns out I'm not the only one who has either rediscovered (or for younger people, discovered for the first time) the appeal of games from the 1980s and 1990s. Though these games had simpler graphics and sound effects, the designers of the games were just as creative as the designers of today, and they were able to overcome the limitations of the hardware of those earlier times and create games that were as challenging and engaging as today's video games. Millions of people play old games using emulation software for DOS programs, Macs, Gameboys, NES, Sega, and other home console, computer, and arcade platforms. And just about every emulator out there has a version that runs on the Raspberry Pi, the marvelous low-cost Linux computer. Even better, a team of passionate retro gaming enthusiasts have created free, labor-of-love software called *RetroPie* that integrates a wide variety of emulators that make it easy to install and play retro-games.

Note   For those of you who might not yet be familiar with the Raspberry Pi, here's a tldr; it's a microcomputer on a printed circuit board about the size of a credit card (or, in the case of the Pi Zero, the size of a stick of gum). It runs a version of the Linux operating system called Raspian, which can be downloaded for free. All you need to run this credit-card-sized computer is a USB keyboard, a microSD card, a USB power supply, an HDMI cable, and a TV or monitor (many of you probably have most of these items already, and if not, you can buy them on the cheap). Don't worry if you have no idea how to use a Raspberry Pi. We'll walk you through the process, step-by-step.

A (Very) Brief History of Video Games

Before we launch into how to get started with retro gaming, let's take a short trip back in time, to the late 1950s, the decade that gave birth to the first video game, so we can gain an appreciation for the early history of video gaming.

Tennis for Two: 1958

Blame it on a physicist named William Higinbotham. He created the first video game in 1958.[2] With a background in atomic bombs, electronics, and radar system displays, Higinbotham was in charge of the instrumentation group at Brookhaven National Laboratory in Upton, New York. (Instrumentation is the term for measurement equipment, such as scales, thermometers, multimeters, signal analyzers, and oscilloscopes.) The laboratory—which conducted research into peacetime uses for nuclear energy—held an annual visitors' day, and thousands of people would flock there each year to learn what the scientists were doing. Brookhaven boasted the first nuclear reactor built after World War II, as well as a particle accelerator called the Cosmotron, which had 288 six-ton magnets to direct particles around its circular storage ring. With attractions like that, Higinbotham knew it would be a challenge to pique people's interest in something as boring as scientific measuring equipment. After thinking about it, he decided it would be fun to make a game that ran on the equipment. He programmed an analog computer to plot arcs of an imaginary ball on the screen of an oscilloscope. He called the game *Tennis for Two* (Figures 1-3 and 1-4). The graphics were extremely primitive, but it set the template for 2D platform games to come. A long horizontal line

---

[2]It could be argued that A S Douglas's 1952 OXO (a tic-tac-toe game) was the first video game, but it didn't have moving graphics, so most people give the honors to Higinbotham.

depicted the ground of a tennis court, and a short vertical line represented the net. A moving blip represented the tennis ball, and players had to press a button at the right time to hit the ball and send it bounding over the net.

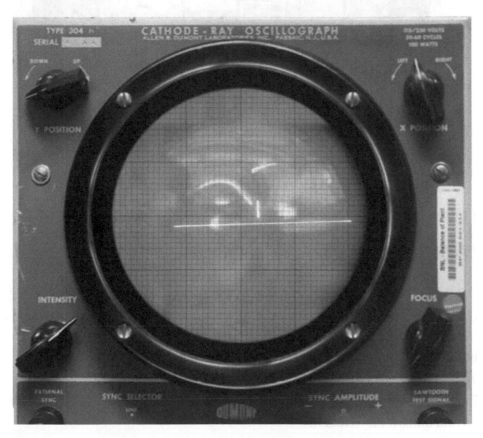

Figure 1-3. William Higinbotham's Tennis for Two game from 1958, considered by many to be the first video game (image Public Domain)

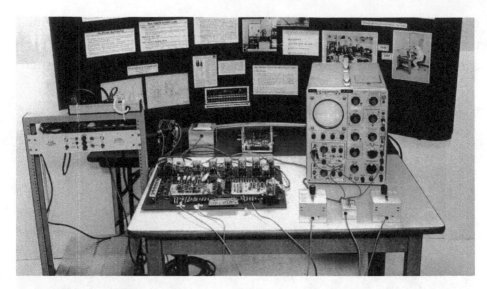

Figure 1-4. *A 1997 recreation of Tennis for Two built for the 50th anniversary celebration of Brookhaven National Laboratory (image Public Domain)*

A knob allowed the player to control the angle of the ball's direction (Figure 1-5). While the game was simple by today's standards, no one had ever seen anything like it. When the ball hit the ground, it would bounce like a real tennis ball. Despite the simplicity of the graphics and controller, *Tennis for Two* proved to be a smashing success, and people formed a long line in front of the display, waiting for the opportunity to virtually whack a virtual ball over a virtual net.

The following year, Higinbotham upgraded *Tennis for Two*, giving players the option to play the game with the gravity level on the Moon and Jupiter as well as Earth. Even though his creation was the hit of Brookhaven's visitors' day for 2 years running, he didn't pursue video games and didn't seek a patent (even though he was awarded over 20 patents for his work in other areas). Nevertheless, Higinbotham's pioneering work, and the public's enthusiastic response to it, foreshadowed the video game revolution of the coming decades.

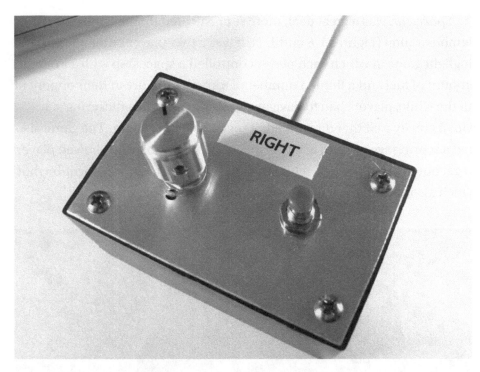

Figure 1-5. *Controller from Windell Oskay's 2008 recreation of Tennis for Two (image Windell Oskay CC BY 2.0)*

Spacewar!: 1962

The next major milestone in video game history was *Spacewar!* created in 1962 by members of the Massachusetts Institute of Technology's Tech Model Railroad Club, led by 25-year-old Steven "Slug" Russell. Unlike *Tennis for Two*, which ran on a custom analog computer, *Spacewar!* ran on a digital computer (a Digital Equipment Corporation PDP-1 minicomputer, which boasted approximately 9,000 bytes of memory) and quickly spread to other academic institutions that had PDP-1 systems, via paper tape with holes punched in it like a player piano roll.

Spacewar! was a great deal, more sophisticated than Higinbotham's demonstration (Figures 1-6 and 1-7). It was a two-player outer-space dogfight game in which each player controlled a spaceship with a limited amount of fuel and a limited number of torpedoes to fire at their opponent. All the while, players had to navigate their ship around a flickering star with a gravity well that threatened to suck the spacecraft in. The game also had a scoring system and a "hyperspace" panic button that allowed players to get out of a tight spot by teleporting their ship to a random location, but which also carried the risk of disintegrating the spacecraft.

Figure 1-6. *Spacewar! on exhibit at the Computer History Museum (image by Kenneth Lu CC BY 2.0)*

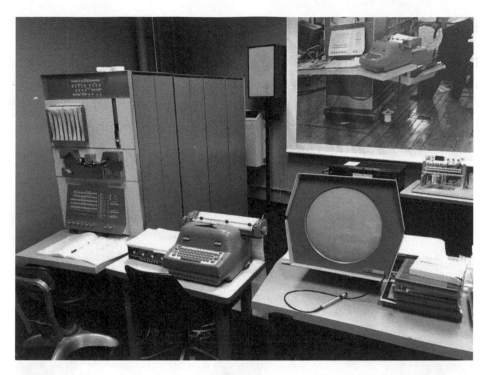

Figure 1-7. *Digital Equipment Corporation PDP-1 minicomputer on display at the Computer History Museum in San Mateo, CA. You can see the storage compartment for the punched paper programming tape attached to the computer case in the upper left. This is how copies of Spacewar! were distributed (image Mark Frauenfelder)*

Early versions of the game required players to flip switches on the computer to play the game, but the students eventually built a handheld gamepad, which had controls for thrust, direction, firing, and hyperspace. It really was a marvelous achievement, especially when you consider that the entire game was only 9k in size. The rockets produced jets of flame when players pressed the thruster button, and the game simulated Newtonian physics, so that the ships continued to move even after the thrusters were deactivated. According to the videogame history site The Dot Eaters, *Spacewar!* was "the foundation of the entire industry and one of the most copied concepts in video game history."

Computer Space: 1971

In 1969, a 26-year-old named Nolan Bushnell, who had played *Spacewar!* in the 1960s as an engineering student at the University of Utah and had worked as the games manager at an amusement park, teamed up with his friend Ted Dabney to make a coin-operated *Spacewar!*-inspired game called *Computer Space* (Figure 1-8).

Figure 1-8. *The first Computer Space arcade cabinet ever made (right) next to another one of Nolan Bushnell's iconic video game co-creations, Pong (image Digital Game Museum CC BY 2.0)*

Instead of using a PDP-1, which cost $120,000 and weighed as much as a VW Beetle, Bushnell and Dabney built the game with custom hardware to bring the cost down. It was the first coin-operated video game and featured a curvaceous molded fiberglass case. In *Computer Space*, the player was pitted against two computer-controlled flying saucers.

Players who successfully destroyed enough flying saucers were allowed to play another round for free. They installed a prototype machine in 1971 at the Dutch Goose bar in Palo Alto, California, and it proved to be a hit with the Stanford crowd who frequented the watering hole. Bushnell and Dabney ended up selling about 1,500 units.

Magnavox Odyssey: 1972

Around the same time, a 50-year-old by the name of Ralph Baer was busy working on a home video game console system. Baer had actually tried to talk his employer, Loral Electronics Corporation, into making a home video game console in the 1950s, but management rebuffed the idea. Baer tried again in the 1960s, and Magnavox finally embraced the concept, releasing the Magnavox Odyssey in 1972 (Figure 1-9). It had no sound effects, and the display was limited to three small squares. It came with plastic overlay sheets with printed graphics that players could attach to their television screen to play six different games, including *Table Tennis*, *Football*, and *Roulette*. Between 1972 and 1975, Magnavox sold 350,000 units, and it kicked off the home video game industry.

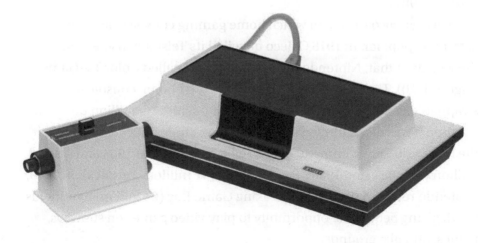

Figure 1-9. *Magnavox Odyssey, the first home video console from 1971 (image by Evan-Amos Public Domain)*

Pong: 1972

Meanwhile, Nolan Bushnell decided that his next game should be simpler than *Computer Space*, which was complex and difficult to learn. The next year, his new company, Atari, released the first video game to become a household word: *Pong*. The two-player ping-pong simulation was a nod to *Tennis for Two*, as well as Odyssey's *Table Tennis* game. *Pong* was a much better seller than *Computer Space*, selling 8,000 units between 1972 and 1974. In 1975, Atari entered the console market with *Home Pong*, which sold 150,000 units in 1975. A great number of *Pong* machines (and clones) appeared in bars, arcades, and home consoles, introducing millions of people to the thrill of moving pixels around on a cathode ray tube.

Video Games Go Mainstream: 1970s–1990s

The era between 1975 and 1981 produced a large number of arcade games now regarded as classics: *Breakout* (1977), *Space Invaders* (1978), *Asteroids* (1979), *Galaxian* (1979), *Pac Man* (1980), *Defender* (1980), *Missile Command* (1980), *Donkey Kong* (1981), *Q*Bert* (1982), *Tempest* (1981), and *Galaga* (1981).

This was also the era in which home gaming consoles became extremely popular. In 1976 Coleco unveiled its Telstar console, and the year after that, Nintendo released a console called Color TV-Game (Figure 1-10). The Atari 2600 (1977) was the first home console to have swappable ROM cartridges and sold an astonishing 30 million units by the time it was discontinued in 1992. The next megahit consoles were the Nintendo Entertainment System, which debuted in 1983 and sold 62 million consoles, and 1988's Sega Genesis (31 million consoles). In 1989, Nintendo released the groundbreaking Game Boy (64 million handhelds sold), giving people the opportunity to play video games on subways, planes, and playgrounds.

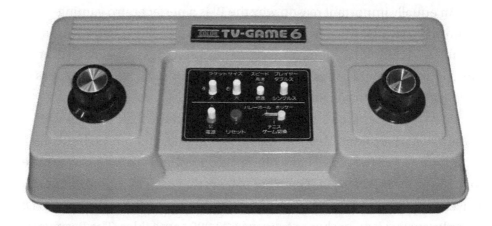

Figure 1-10. *Nintendo's first home video console from 1977, the Color TV-Game 6 (image Chapuisat/MagentaGreen CC BY 2.0)*

The increasing popularity of home computers in the 1980s meant that people now could play a variety of games on the Apple II, the Commodore 64, the Atari ST, and the IBM PC.

Note   The most popular game console in history is Sony's PlayStation 2, which was released in 2000 and sold over 155 million consoles. The bestselling handheld is the Nintendo DS, which came out in 2004 and has sold 154 million units to date.

The Raspberry Pi Retro Gaming Community

The Raspberry Pi is an ideal platform for retro-games because it's inexpensive, easy to configure, and tiny. It draws very little electricity but has enough processing power to run most arcade, PC, and console games from the 1970s to 1990s (and beyond, but not without some lags and glitches). Because of these attributes, the Pi is the most versatile computing platform ever created.

An equally important reason why the Pi is a perfect retro gaming platform is because once people discovered what the Raspberry Pi was capable of, it didn't take long for them to start creating and porting over emulators that could run on the Pi, as well as building hardware such as buttons, joysticks, power supplies, cases, and displays.

Retro gaming enthusiasts are using the Pi to make a dizzying variety of game playing hardware. There are miniature handheld players no bigger than a car remote. On the other end of the spectrum, there are full-sized arcade machines powered by a Pi. There are players that fit in an Altoids mint tin, players that look like the Game Boys (as seen in Figure 1-11) and Nintendo DS, and players that let you choose from over 20,000 game titles. The Raspberry Pi retro gaming community is huge and very active. There are emulators for every platform imaginable, and many models of handhelds and consoles available online to download and make on a 3D printer or laser cutter.

Figure 1-11. *Two versions of the Pocket PiGRRL, made from Raspberry open source 3D printed cases, and hardware manufactured by adafruit.com (image Adafruit/Ruiz Brothers CC BY-SA 3.0)*

We'll cover the basic hardware needed to get up and running in the following chapters, but for now, let's take a look at the two kinds of software that make retro gaming possible on the Pi—emulators and roms.

Emulators

An emulator is a virtual computer that runs on a computer. Modern computers are so much more powerful than earlier computers that they can emulate them very easily. For example, the DOSBox program I use to play *Wizardry* is a virtual MS-DOS machine that runs on a Raspberry Pi. (There are also versions of DOSBox that run in Linux, Mac OS X, and Windows.) The Raspberry Pi has more horsepower than most computers and consoles from the 1990s, making it ideal for running emulators.

There are two main retro gaming emulation platforms for the Raspberry Pi: RetroPie and RecalBox. Both systems are excellent and allow you to play tens of thousands of classic games on the Pi. In general, RecalBox is a bit simpler to set up and use, and RetroPie has more options for customization. In this book, I'm going to use RetroPie for the projects, but the chapters that show you how to make a retro gaming console, arcade machine, and handheld will work with either platform. Try them both and see which one you prefer.

Let's Talk About ROMs

You're undoubtedly familiar with game cartridges (Figures 1-12 and 1-13). If you were to crack open the plastic case on one, you'd find a small printed circuit board with a number of chips mounted on it. One of those chips is a read-only memory (ROM) chip that contains the executable game program.

Figure 1-12. *A collection of cartridges for the Nintendo DS and 3DS. The cartridges have read-only memory (ROM) chips that store the programs that run the games (image Mark Frauenfelder)*

Figure 1-13. *Inside the Super Mario Land 2: 6 Golden Coins game cartridge (image by Thomy_pc—Own work, Copyrighted free use, Wikimedia.org)*

Game enthusiasts learned how to back up their games by downloading a copy of the data stored on the ROM chip (and on the proprietary hardware of arcade machines, too, but the process is more involved) and saving them on their computer. Today, you can buy hardware to download copies of cartridge ROM files (the process is called *dumping*) and keep them safely stored on a hard drive or thumb drive. But more interestingly, you can use emulation software to run copies of ROM files (more casually written in lowercase as *roms*) on your home computer or Raspberry Pi.

Caution   It must be noted that many ROM files are copyrighted and that game publishers have started shutting down web sites offering roms. It's still trivially easy to find roms for almost any game you want. But you should be aware that of the risks involved with downloading roms from the Internet. If you don't already own a legitimate copy of a game, it's definitely illegal to download the rom, and especially illegal to share copies of the rom with other people. What about downloading a rom of a game you already own? That depends on who you ask. Nintendo's legal FAQ states, "Whether you have an authentic game or not…it is illegal to download and play a Nintendo ROM from the Internet." Is Nintendo correct? Professor Derek Bambauer, who teaches Internet law at the University of Arizona, told Howtogeek.com that the law is not as cut-and-dry as Nintendo would like you to believe. "If I own a copy of Super Mario World, I can play it whenever I want," he said, "but what I'd really like to do is play it on my phone or my laptop." If you download a rom, he says, "You're not giving the game to anybody else, you're just playing a game you already own on your phone. The argument would be there's no market harm here; that it's not substituting for a purchase. This is by no means a slam-dunk argument. But it's by no means a silly one." OK, then what about using one of those devices that sucks the rom out of a cartridge you own so you can play it on an emulator? Nintendo says even that is against the law. Bambauer argues that it's a gray area. There's a potential fair use argument for making a copy of your cartridge, but it isn't that much different from downloading a copy from the Internet. "In both cases what you're doing is creating an additional copy." There are, however, two ways to play games on an emulator without worrying about the long arm of the law swooping you up and throwing you in prison. One way to play old games legally is with a USB hardware device like the Retrode (about $85), which lets you plug in your carts and play them with emulation software. Another way is play games that are legal to download as roms. This page (`https://retropie.org.uk/forum/topic/10918/where-to-legally-acquire-content-to-play-on-retropie`) has a list of legal roms to get you started. Yet another way to play games on the Pi is to write your own, which is a topic we'll touch on later in the book. And, in 2018, SEGA made many of its roms available with the purchase of its games on the Steam platform.

Summary

Since the birth of gaming, computer technology has always granted us a better experience in audiovisual immersion. Each succeeding generation of computer technology leaves behind the last. Many of our first memories of video gaming are long forgotten due to the fundamental adoption of always improving technology. But many of us hold onto our first exposure with gaming and recall it as the best of times. Fortunately for us, modern-day technology has granted the ability to relive many of these first gaming memories on modern machines. The exponential advancement of processing power has opened the doors to emulate video games and hardware lost to time. Modern-day priorities like cost, power, efficiency, and economies of scale have gifted us what is likely the most popular computer from here forward: the do-all, open platform computer called the Raspberry Pi, a single-board computer that has established a household name in reliving retro video game memories of lost and forgotten hardware.

CHAPTER 2

Setting Up the Raspberry Pi for Retro Gaming

There's no denying that the Raspberry Pi is one of the most underpowered computers on the market today. Even the highest-end model, the 3B+, is many times slower than an entry-level laptop with an Intel Core i7 monitor (Figure 2-1). But what this single board lacks in horsepower it more than makes up for in affordability, compactness, simplicity, and fun. The least expensive flavor of Pi, the itty-bitty Zero, costs just $5, while the feature-filled 3B+ (mainly featured in this book), smaller than a deck of playing cards, will set you back a whopping $35. Users with the need of more of multi-application desktop environment have a solution with the Raspberry Pi 4. The Pi 4 includes the option to selection the installed onboard RAM in 1GB, 2GB, or 4GB configurations with a price ceiling of only $55. All Pi 4 models include dual micro-HDMI ports for 4k display output and USB 3.0 support. A Pi can easily run 8-bit and 16-bit console games (there *are* emulators for Nintendo 64 and Sega Dreamcast, but the experience is subpar).

© Mark Frauenfelder and Ryan Bates 2019
M. Frauenfelder and R. Bates, *Raspberry Pi Retro Gaming*,
https://doi.org/10.1007/978-1-4842-5153-9_2

Figure 2-1. *Three different models of the Raspberry Pi. Left: Pi 1 from 2011. Middle: Pi 3 Model B V1.2. Right: Pi Zero W V1.1 (image Mark Frauenfelder)*

The Raspberry Pi is a fully functional computer. It runs the Linux operating system. Even though it is relatively weak in comparison with modern computers, it's a powerhouse compared to the personal computers of the 1980s. I remember buying a Dell PC in the late 1980s which came with what I thought was a huge amount of RAM—a whopping 640k. And at the time, it *was* a lot. My Apple II had just 64k of RAM, which I upgraded with an expansion card (costing a few hundred dollars) to 128k. The Raspberry Pi 3 B+ has 1GB RAM. If someone had shown me the Pi in 1987, it would have seemed like alien technology, and I would have guessed it might cost over $10,000. The Pi is a good example of Moore's law, which states that the transistor density of computer chips doubles every 18 months. The nonstop progress of technology never ceases to amaze me.

The Pi was created in 2006 by a group of educators, engineers, and enthusiasts who wanted to make a computer for kids that offered the same kind of openness to exploration and creativity that computers in the 1980s had. In those pre-Web days, computers came with a built-in BASIC compiler, and people often wrote their own games and other programs from scratch. The Pi is a return to those creative days. Its default operating system has a number of programming languages preinstalled on it, including Scratch and Python. People have used Raspberry Pis to make cameras, touch-screen tablets, home automation systems, weather stations, Internet radio stations, home entertainment systems, control systems for satellites, and experimental platforms on the International Space Station.

When I received my first Raspberry Pi about 5 years ago, I set it up as a *Minecraft* server. I spent an entire weekend looking at instructions posted by other people who had figured out how to do it, and when I finally succeeded, I emailed all my friends who played *Minecraft* (and had kids who played it, too) and invited them to sign up. In a matter of minutes, a half-dozen people were building and digging in the *Minecraft* universe running on my Raspberry Pi. The next day, my friend sent me a text message to tell me that his son was connected to the *Minecraft* server while they were flying to Ohio on a Wi-Fi-enabled passenger jet. I looked at the little $35 Raspberry Pi on my desk and marveled at the fact that a laptop computer 1,000 miles away and 30,000 feet in the air was communicating with my Raspberry Pi. We really are living in the future, I thought.

Raspberry Pi: The Nuts and Bolts

Let's take a closer look at the latest version of the Raspberry Pi, the Model 3 B+ (Figure 2-2), to learn a little more about how it works.

Figure 2-2. *The Raspberry Pi 3 Model B+ (image Gareth Halfacree CC BY-SA 2.0)*

USB Ports—There are four USB 2.0 ports. They can be used to connect peripherals, like mice, keyboards, controllers, and flash drives. You can also use them to provide power to devices, but don't expect them to power a display, unless it's very small.

GPIO Pins—GPIO stands for General Purpose Input Pins. These 40 pins are sometimes called the GPIO header, and you use them to connect your Pi to other circuits and devices. The pins have different functions. Some of them supply 5 volts, some supply 3 volts, and others can be configured to send or receive digital and analog signals. These pins will come in handy when we build our projects! Be wary! These GPIO pins have a direct connection to the Pi's main CPU! Any mishandling of voltage or current here can cripple the Pi.

MicroSD Card Slot—Your desktop or laptop computer has a hard drive to store data, applications, and the operating system. The Pi uses a microSD card like a hard drive.

Ethernet Port—The Pi has an Ethernet port, which can come in handy when setting up the built-in Wi-Fi. You probably won't need to use

Ethernet for retro-computing, but it is faster than Wi-Fi; so if you don't mind having an Ethernet cable emanating from your Pi, it's a perfectly reasonable way to connect to the Internet.

A/V Out—This TRRS (Tip, Ring, Ring, Sleeve) connector is the same size as 3.5mm headphone jack. The difference here- in addition to the left and right audio channels this connector also houses composite video output. If you plug an unpowered speaker into this jack, the audio will be very low. We'll show you how to get around this limitation later in the book. This jack can also be used to connect to an analog video source that accepts RCA jacks (the yellow, red, white connections). If you truly want that CRT scanline feel, this option is for you.

HDMI Port—Most TV sets and computer displays have HDMI ports, which makes it dead simple to connect your Pi to one. If your monitor or TV set has a speaker, you can output digital audio to that device and ignore the analog audio jack.

Bluetooth—The Pi 3 B+ has a Bluetooth radio, which means you can connect wireless controllers to it. Hurray! We'll show you how to connect them later in the book.

Wi-Fi—The Wi-Fi radio comes in very handy, because it allows you to add roms and additional emulators to your Pi without having to plug in an Ethernet cable or a USB stick. Many handheld player designs for the Pi don't have an easy way to access the Ethernet or USB ports, so Wi-Fi is essential.

MicroUSB Port—The MicroUSB port is for supplying power to the Pi. It doesn't have data lines.

Keeping Things Cool

Computers generate heat, just like any electrical appliance. The Pi is designed to withstand high temperatures, but if the CPU/GPU chip gets too hot (the official operational maximum is 85° C), it will protect itself by slowing down. If your Pi starts to overheat, you'll see a yellow square or thermometer appear in the top right of your display. And if the temperature starts creeping into the maximum temperature zone, the square or thermometer will turn red.

It's important to allow your Pi to dissipate excess heat, especially if you overclock the processor to make it run faster. The simplest way to cool the chip is to allow ambient air to come into contact with the CPU/GPU chip. That means having vent holes in the case. If that's still not sufficient to keep the temperature down, you can attach a heatsink to the Pi's CPU/GPU chip. Still too hot? Then you can add a small fan to blow air over the heatsink.

Tip   To see the CPU core temperature of your Pi, open a terminal window and enter the command `vcgencmd measure_temp`. It will return an output that looks like something like this: `temp=47.8'C`

Heatsinks—A heatsink is typically made of aluminum and is attached to the Pi's CPU/GPU with thermally conductive glue or tape. The heatsink has fins, which effectively increases the surface area of the CPU to allow the heat it generates to be transferred to air moving past it as well as through radiation. Heatsinks for the Pi are inexpensive—you can get them for $1 or less. Don't expect heatsinks to make a big difference in temperature—they'll only drop the temperature of the CPU/GPU chip a couple of degrees centigrade.

Fans—If you're really concerned about controlling the temperature of your Pi, you'll need a small fan to blow air across the fins of the heatsink. As active devices, fans can make a big difference in the CPU/GPU core temperature, keeping it well below the operational maximum temperature. Adafruit.com sells a miniature 5V cooling fan that can be powered from the GPIO pins for $3.50.

A Bare-Bones Retro Gaming Setup

The Pi is a full computer, but you can't do anything with it other than admire it until you supply it with power and attach some peripherals to it. Here's a rundown of what you need, at a minimum, to play retro-games on the Pi.

Tip   You can buy kits that have most or all of the following components at a price that's competitive with buying them all separately. But if you already have some of the components, you'll save money by buying only the things you need.

- **Raspberry Pi**: Any model will work, but I recommend a Raspberry Pi 3 Model B + ($35), which will happily run most retro games you throw at it. The Pi 3's standard size HDMI port is more common to interface with than the Pi 4's micro HDMI ports. (Hold off on getting a Pi Zero for now, because it doesn't have standard-size ports.)

- **Laptop or desktop computer**: You'll use your computer to install the RetroPie software onto the microSD card.

- **Keyboard**: Even if you only ever play games with a gamepad, it's a good idea to have a USB keyboard so you can configure the Pi. Also, if you play PC, C64, Mac, or other computer games, you'll need a keyboard to play them. I'll bet you can scrounge up a keyboard for free somewhere, but if you need to buy one, Amazon sells them for about $14 (including a mouse).

- **Speakers or headphones**: You can use headphones or a set of powered speakers to connect to the Raspberry Pi's 3.5mm jack. If you're using a TV, the HDMI connection will send audio to the TV's speakers as well.

- **MicroSD card**: I recommend getting a microSD card with at least 32GB, so you can load it with tons of game files. Jeff Geerling ran speed tests on a bunch of different microSD cards and found that certain brands can read and write data almost four times faster than others (the Samsung 32GB Evo+ ($14) is the fastest) (`www.pidramble.com/wiki/benchmarks/microsd-cards`).

- **SD card adapter and/or USB card reader**: If your computer has an SD card slot built into it, you can insert the microSD card into it. Almost all microSD cards are sold with an adapter. If your computer doesn't have an SD card slot, you'll need a USB card reader. They cost about $10 and most have a slot for an SD card and a microSD card. See Figure 2-3.

- **Micro USB cable/USB power supply**: If you are like me, you'll have a bunch of these lying around. If not, they are cheap. Be sure to get a 5V power supply that has 2.5A. If you've decided to use a Raspberry Pi 4, you will need a USB-C power supply capable of outputting 15watts.

- **HDMI cable**: Again, you probably have one lying around, or someone you know does. If not, go to your favorite online superstore and buy one for under $10.

- **HDMI display**: For now, use your TV set or a computer monitor. We will discuss display options in the project build chapters later in the book.

- **USB Gamepad**: To start out, try the Buffalo "iBuffalo Classic USB Gamepad," modeled after the original SNES controller. They are usually about $20 and will let you play Gameboy, NES, SNES, and SEGA Genesis games. If you want to get started with a wireless gamepad, anything from 8BitDo.com is a good choice.

Figure 2-3. *The upper left is a microSD card with the included SD card adapter. The bottom left is a USB adapter that accepts SD cards and microSD cards. The white circle on the Raspberry Pi indicates the slot for the microSD card*

Once you have everything, it's time to install RetroPie.

Installing RetroPie onto Your Raspberry Pi

There are two versions of RetroPie available, one for the Raspberry Pi Zero and Raspberry Pi 1 and one for the Raspberry Pi 2 and the Raspberry Pi 3. To install, follow these steps.

1. On your computer, download the version of RetroPie that works with the Pi you are using from https://retropie.org.uk/download (see Figure 2-4). The file is about 700 MB, so depending on your Internet service provider's speed, it could take several minutes to download.

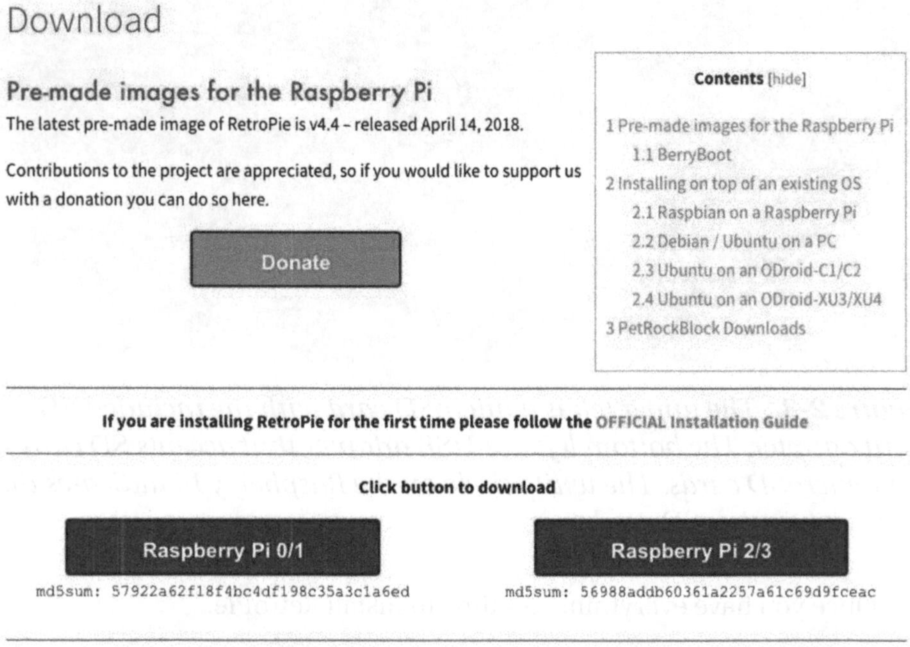

Download

Pre-made images for the Raspberry Pi

The latest pre-made image of RetroPie is v4.4 – released April 14, 2018.

Contributions to the project are appreciated, so if you would like to support us with a donation you can do so here.

Donate

Contents [hide]

1 Pre-made images for the Raspberry Pi
  1.1 BerryBoot
2 Installing on top of an existing OS
  2.1 Raspbian on a Raspberry Pi
  2.2 Debian / Ubuntu on a PC
  2.3 Ubuntu on an ODroid-C1/C2
  2.4 Ubuntu on an ODroid-XU3/XU4
3 PetRockBlock Downloads

If you are installing RetroPie for the first time please follow the OFFICIAL Installation Guide

Click button to download

Raspberry Pi 0/1

md5sum: 57922a62f18f4bc4df198c35a3c1a6ed

Raspberry Pi 2/3

md5sum: 56988addb60361a2257a61c69d9fceac

Figure 2-4. *Download page for RetroPie*

2. The downloaded file will have a name similar to
    this: `retropie-4.4-rpi2_rpi3.img.gz`. The "gz"
    extension means that the file was compressed with
    the GNU zip (gzip) compression algorithm. You'll
    need to unzip the file. If you are using Windows,
    you can use the free 7-Zip utility from `7-zip.org`.
    On the Mac, you can use the Terminal app. It's in
    `Applications/Utilities/Terminal.app`. Enter
    `gunzip` followed by a blank space, then use your
    mouse to drag the `.gz` file into the `Terminal` window
    (Figure 2-5). Press Enter and the file will unzip.

Note   PC users can download the utility Win32DiskImager. Much of
these steps are similar in a Window's environment.

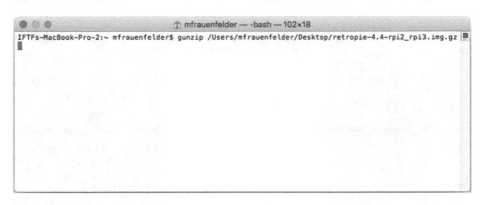

Figure 2-5. *Unzipping RetroPie in the Macintosh Terminal window*

3. Now it's time to flash the RetroPie image to the
    SD card. An easy way to do this is with a free
    utility called Etcher. The web site (`www.balena.
    io/etcher/`) has versions for Mac, Windows, and

Linux. Pick the version you need from the pull-
down menu, download it, then double-click the
downloaded file to install it on your computer.

4. Put the microSD card into the SD adapter or the USB
    card reader and insert into the SD slot or USB port of
    your computer.

5. In Etcher, click Select image then navigate to the
    unzipped RetroPie image on your computer. Then
    click Select drive and click the microSD card.

Tip   If you see a message that says the file is "Locked" (Figure 2-6),
that means the small slider switch on the SD card adapter is set to
write-protect. Just pull the adapter out of your computer, slide the
switch, and reinsert it into your computer.

Figure 2-6. *If the slider switch on your SD card adapter is locked,
you'll see this message*

6. Click `Flash!` You may get a pop-up asking you to
    enter your computer password. Go ahead and enter
    it. It will take up to 10 minutes to flash and validate
    the image. See Figure 2-7.

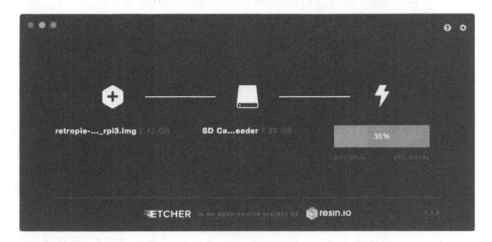

Figure 2-7. *Use Etcher to install RetroPie on a microSD card*

7. Remove the microSD card and insert it into the
    microSD slot on the Raspberry Pi. Attach the
    monitor, USB keyboard, and gamepad to the Pi.

8. Once everything is plugged in, power up the Pi by
    plugging in the micro USB power supply. You should
    see a row of Raspberry Pi icons appear on the display.
    (If you are using the Pi 3 Model B+, there will be four
    raspberries, signifying a quad-core CPU). After that,
    you'll see a series of lines of text and graphics appear,
    including the EmulationStation and RetroPie opening
    screens. Finally, you'll see a white box that says
    `WELCOME. 1 GAMEPAD DETECTED. HOLD A BUTTON ON`
    `YOUR DEVICE TO CONFIGURE IT. PRESS F4 TO QUIT`
    `AT ANY TIME.`

9. Hold any button on your USB gamepad. After a
    couple of seconds, the display will report back
    with information about the kind of gamepad you
    have. Now, it will walk you through the process of
    configuring the buttons, as shown in Figure 2-8.
    It will first ask you to press the D-pad Up button.
    As soon as you do, it will ask you to press the D-pad
    Down button. Continue until you've configured all
    the buttons on your gamepad. If you run out of
    buttons before you reach the end of the list, just
    press and hold any key to skip to the next item on
    the list. For HOTKEY ENABLE, I recommend using
    the SELECT key on your gamepad (the Configuring
    window will likely describe it as BUTTON 6, as shown
    in Figure 2-9).

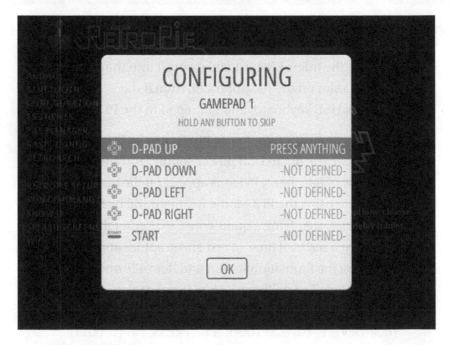

Figure 2-8. Configuring your gamepad

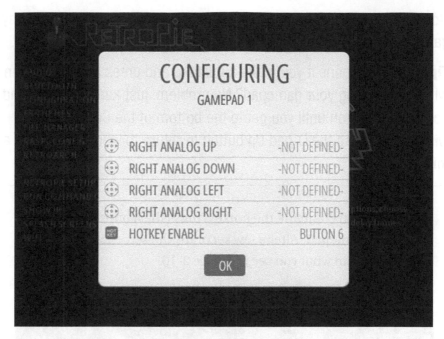

Figure 2-9. *If you configure the SELECT key to be the HOTKEY ENABLE trigger, it will probably be displayed as button 6*

Tip   The hotkey allows you to perform different actions using a controller with the emulators included in RetroPie. If you configured the SELECT button as your hotkey enabler, here is a list of the hotkey functions:

Select+Start	Exit
Select+Right Shoulder	Save Game State
Select+Left Shoulder	Load Saved Game State
Select+Right	Input State Slot Increase
Select+Left	Input State Slot Decrease
Select+X	RGUI Menu
Select+B	Reset

Note   The A button on its own is used to select menu items and play games in RetroPie. The B button backs out to the higher-level menu.

Tip   What happens if you make a mistake and press a wrong button while configuring your gamepad? No problem, just keep pressing and holding any button until you get to the bottom of the Configuration window, then use the D-pad Up button to return to where you made a mistake.

10.   After you configure the hotkey, press the A button on your gamepad. After a few seconds, the screen will change to what you see in Figure 2-10.

Figure 2-10. When you are finished configuring your gamepad, you'll return to the MAIN MENU

11. Press B and use the D-pad to scroll to the
     RASPI-CONFIG option (Figure 2-11). Press A.

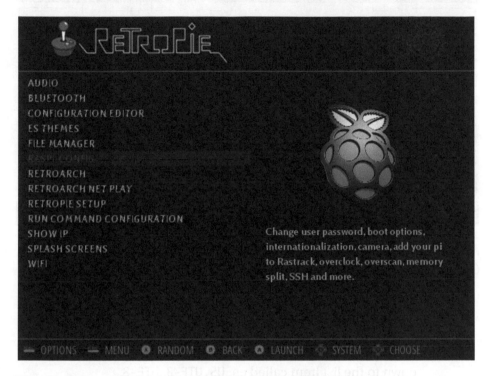

Figure 2-11. *The RASPI-CONFIG option in the RetroPie setup menu*

12. Using the keyboard, scroll down to LOCALISATION
     OPTIONS. Press the Enter or Return key on your
     keyboard. There are four menu items in this section:
     Change Locale, Change Timezone, Change
     Keyboard Layout, and Change Wi-Fi Country
     (Figure 2-12).

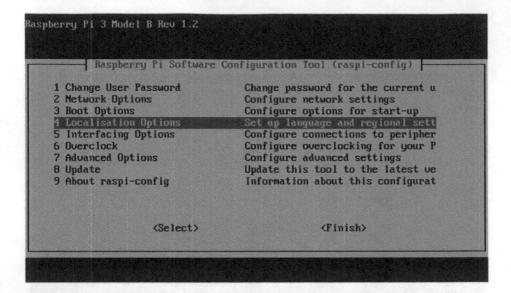

Figure 2-12. *You will set up your Pi and keyboard in Localisation Options*

13. Select Change Local. The list of locales is arranged
    in alphabetical order by language followed by
    country. For instance, if you want US English, scroll
    down to the list item called en_US.UTF-8 UTF-8.
    (No matter what locale you choose, pick the UTF-
    8 version.) If your keyboard has a pagedown key,
    you can use it to quickly move through the many
    locales on the list. Select your local by pressing the
    space bar (Figure 2-13). Then press the Tab key until
    <OK> is highlighted. Press Enter on your keyboard.
    You may be asked to further refine your selection.
    Highlight the language you want and continue.

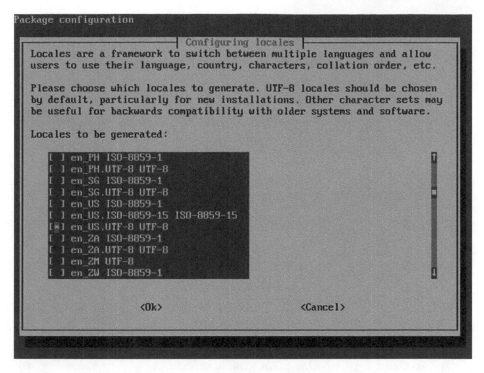

Figure 2-13. *In this screenshot, US English has been selected*

14. Select LOCALISATION OPTIONS again, and select
    Change Timezone. Highlight your geographic area,
    highlight the time zone, then highlight <OK> and
    press Enter.

15. Select LOCALISATION OPTIONS again and configure
    the keyboard and layout you are using in the Change
    Keyboard Layout menu item. If you don't know what
    kind of keyboard you have, it's a safe bet to go with
    one of the Generic PC options. You'll then be asked
    to choose the layout of your keyboard. If you are
    using a US English keyboard, you'll first have to select
    Other at the bottom of the list, then select English
    (US). Then scroll up to select the English (US)

keyboard layout (as opposed to Dvorak or other
alternate layouts) as shown in Figure 2-14. You will
be asked to configure a couple of other options. Just
choose the defaults.

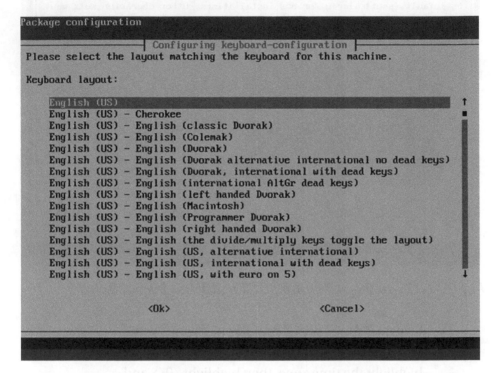

Figure 2-14. *Select English (US) to use a standard QWERTY layout*

16. Select LOCALISATION OPTIONS again. Open Change
    Wi-Fi Country and select your country. Use the
    Page Down button on your keyboard to quickly
    scroll to your country.

17. Return to the Raspberry Pi Software Configuration
    Tool menu (Figure 2-15) and select <Finish>. If you
    are asked to reboot, select <Yes>. You'll be returned
    to the RetroPie configuration screen.

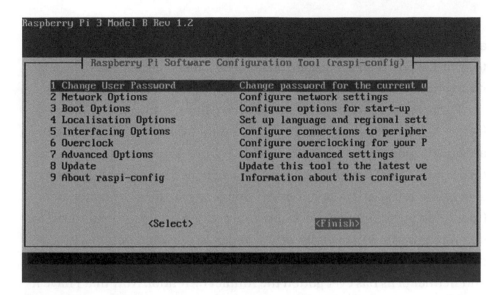

Figure 2-15. *Use the Tab key on your keyboard to highlight <Finish> then press Enter*

18. Use the D-pad to scroll down to WIFI. Choose the same Wi-Fi network that your main computer is connected to and enter the password.

19. Select <Exit> to return to the RetroPie configuration screen.

Congratulations! Your Raspberry Pi has been set up to start playing games! In the next section, we'll install a retro-game so you can check your setup.

Installing Your First Rom

As I mentioned earlier, even though almost every retro-game rom file imaginable is a Google search away, if you don't want to violate someone's copyright, you'll need to use game files you have a right to use.

In 2018, Sega made a bunch of their games available through Steam, and fortunately, it includes the uncompressed roms so you can add them to your Raspberry Pi. A package of about 59 games sells for $30. Learn more about it here: https://store.steampowered.com/sub/102625/.

For now, let's install one of my favorite games, a dungeon crawler from the early 1980s called *Rogue*. In this public domain DOS game, you are an adventurer seeking the Amulet of Yendor. You must fight your way through multiple descending levels, each of which is randomly generated every time you start a new game. The dungeons are filled with monsters (identified by the letters A–Z), traps, gold coins, food (it's easy to starve to death in this game!), weapons, armor, magic scrolls, and potions. It's a very difficult game. My sister and I spent countless hours playing it in the 1980s, and neither of us has ever gotten the Amulet of Yendor. Now that I have it on my Pi, I've spent too much time giving it another try.

To play DOS games on RetroPie, you first need to install a DOS emulator, because RetroPie doesn't include one in the image file. The most popular DOS emulator is DOSBox. Here's how to install it.

Installing DOSBox on RetroPie

Make sure your Pi is connected to Wi-Fi. You can do this from the main RetroPie menu. Then follow these steps.

1. From the same menu, select RetroPie Setup.

2. Select the menu item called Update RetroPie-Setup script.

3. After it fetches the latest version of the setup script, select Manage packages, then Manage optional packages, then scroll down to dosbox. Select it, then select Install from binary. It could take a few minutes for the installation to complete.

Note   As you can see, the Manage optional packages has a lot of other different emulators for different gaming platforms available. If you know you are going to be playing games using one of these emulators, you can install them now.

4. Select the <Back> three times until you return to the RetroPie Setup Script menu, and select Perform reboot. Allow the Pi to reboot.

5. When the Pi reboots, you'll see that you now have an MS-DOS emulator in EmulationStation (Figure 2-16).

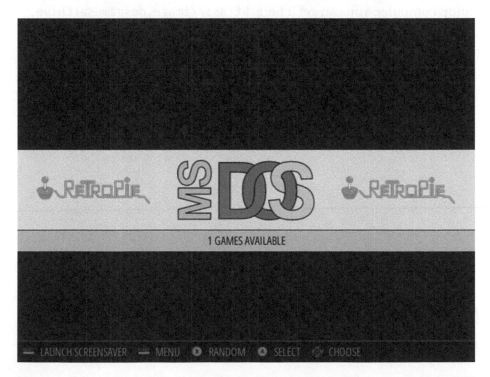

Figure 2-16. *After installing DOSBox, RetroPie will have an MS DOS item in the carousel*

Tip There's a lot of good information about DOSBox here: `https://github.com/retropie/retropie-setup/wiki/PC`, including a list of the compatibility of DOS games running on the DOSBox emulator.

Installing Rogue on RetroPie

There are a number of ways to install a game in the microSD card on your Pi. We'll cover the two most common ways to do it.

But first, you need to download a copy of *Rogue* to your desktop or laptop computer. You can get it here: `https://image.dosgamesarchive.com/games/rogue.zip`. Unzip it and you'll find three files, as shown in Figure 2-17.

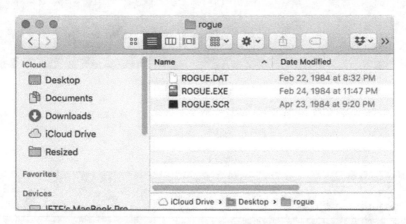

Figure 2-17. *Unzip the file with your unarchiving utility*

Option 1: USB Memory Stick

Insert a flash drive into your PC or Mac. On the flash drive, create a folder called retropie.

Note   It helps to have a USB thumb drive with an LED on it so you can tell when it's finished writing.

Eject the flash drive from your computer and insert it into a USB slot on the Raspberry Pi. Wait for it to copy the existing contents of the roms directory on the Pi to the flash drive. If your flash drive has an LED, wait for it to start blinking. Otherwise, give it about 3 minutes before moving on to the next step.

Pull out the flash drive and insert it back into your computer. Open the retropie folder you created, and you'll see that it has been populated with three new folders: BIOS, configs, and roms (see Figure 2-18). Open the roms folder and scroll down until you see pc. Copy the *rogue* folder on your computer into the pc folder.

Eject the flash drive from your computer and insert it in your Pi. The rogue folder will automatically be copied to the pc folder on the Pi's microSD card.

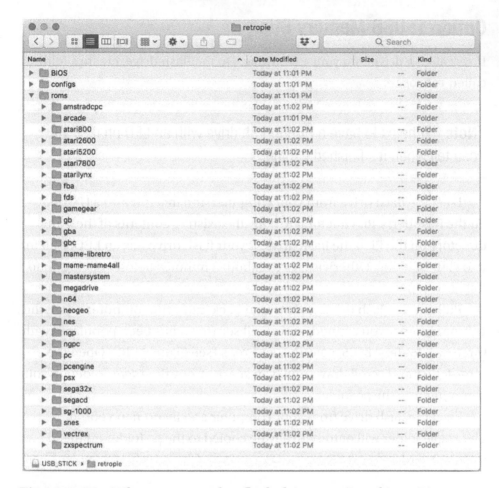

Figure 2-18. *When you attach a flash drive to a Raspberry Pi running RetroPie, it will sync rom, bios, and configuration files between the Pi's microSD card and the flash drive*

Option 2: Network Transfer

Transferring files over a home network using Wi-Fi is easy, and I prefer it over the flash drive method mentioned earlier because it's faster and doesn't require using a USB flash drive.

The first thing you should do is change the default password (raspberry) on your Pi, because after it's connected to the Internet, it becomes a target for hackers, and raspberry is the first password they'll try. Use your gamepad to scroll to the RetroPie icon in the carousel and select RASPI-CONFIG by pressing A. This will run the Raspberry Pi Software Configuration Tool. From this window, select the first menu item, Change User Password. You'll be asked to Enter new UNIX password. Make a note of your new password.

Now that you have a new password, you'll need to enable something called SSH (Secure Shell), which allows you to access the files in the Pi's microSD card from another computer, as long as both are on the same Wi-Fi or Ethernet connection. From the main RetroPie menu, select RASPI-CONFIG again.

Select the menu item called Interfacing Options. Select SSH. You'll be asked if you would like the SSH server to be enabled. Answer Yes.

Once you have received confirmation that SSH has been installed, you can reboot by pressing the Start button on your controller, scrolling to QUIT, and selecting RESTART EMULATIONSTATION.

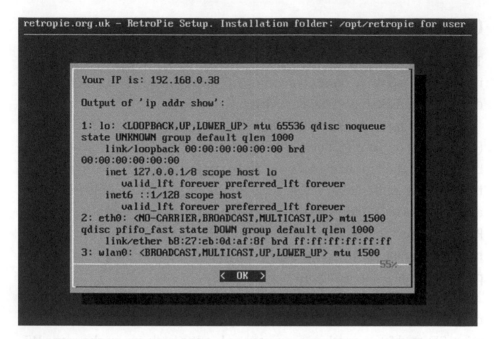

Figure 2-19. *Of the many ways to find out what your Raspberry Pi's IP address is, selecting SHOW IP from the RetroPie Setup icon is the easiest*

On the main RetroPie options window, scroll down to SHOW IP. The first line of the results will show you the IP address of the Raspberry Pi. Make a note of the number. As you can see in Figure 2-19, my Pi's IP address is 192.168.0.38. Yours will probably be different. (This is not a permanent address, and it may be different the next time you start up your Pi.)

Now, depending on whether you have a Mac or PC, follow the applicable instructions to continue.

Network Transfer on a Mac

On a Mac, go to Finder and press cmd-K. This will open a window called Connect to Server. See Figure 2-20. Enter the IP address as shown in the Server Address field as shown earlier (your IP address will probably be different).

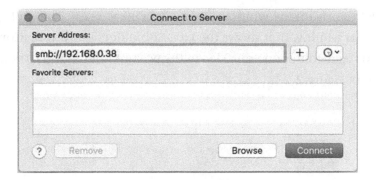

Figure 2-20. *Connecting to your Pi via SSH*

Tip   You may be able to skip entering the IP address by entering
smb://retropie instead. I've had mixed results using this method.

Connect as Guest (Figure 2-21).

Figure 2-21. *Connecting as Guest*

Select roms from the window that loads (Figure 2-22). This will open a new finder window that shows the roms subfolders on your Pi. Copy the unzipped rogue folder on your Mac to the pc subfolder in the roms folder, as shown in Figure 2-23.

Figure 2-22. *Select the roms volume*

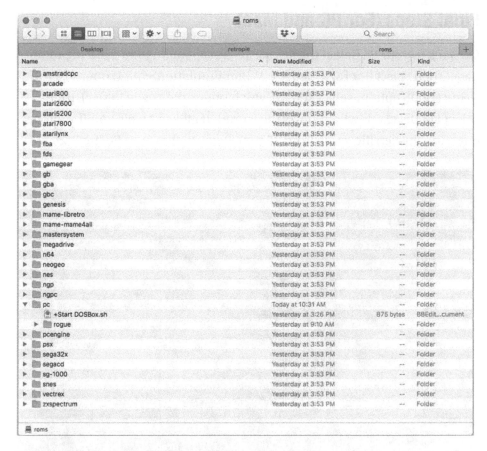

Figure 2-23. *This is a remote connection to the subfolders in the roms folder on your Raspberry Pi's microSD card*

Network Transfer on a Windows Computer

From a File Explorer window, enter \\ip address (in my case, that was \\192.168.0.38). If you are asked for your username and password, enter the ones for your Pi. (You can also try \\retropie which often works.)

You'll see a number of folders. Open the roms folder. Copy the unzipped rogue folder on your Windows machine to the pc subfolder in the roms folder.

Final Steps (For PC and Mac)

Go back to your Pi. Select the RetroPie Setup menu item from the main page, then select Perform reboot. When EmulationStation opens, scroll to the MSDOS option, select ROGUE (which opens the rogue folder), then select ROGUE again (which starts the game). If all went well, you'll soon be enjoying this terrific game from 25 years ago, as shown in Figure 2-24.

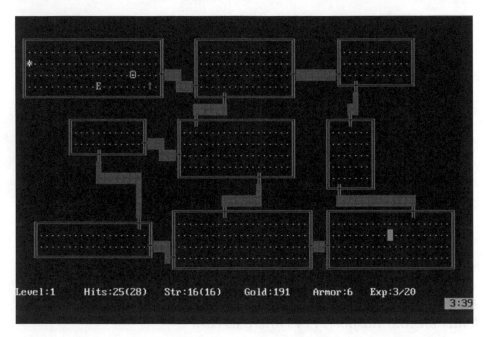

Figure 2-24. *Every level in Rogue is procedurally generated*

Summary

Congratulations! You've now got RetroPie running with your first game. A whole world of retro gaming excitement awaits. In the next chapter, we'll go deeper into the RetroPie platform and how to configure it for your particular needs.

CHAPTER 3

A Closer Look at RetroPie

RetroPie is an emulator operating system that integrates a number of retro gaming projects. RetroPie itself sits above Raspbian, a flavor of Linux written for the Raspberry Pi. It neatly combines two popular emulator front ends, RetroArch and EmulationStation. RetroPie is a feature-rich platform with many options for customization. In this section, we'll go a bit deeper into its capabilities.

To explore RetroPie's options, you should have a keyboard, mouse, and gamepad controller. You also need to make sure your Raspberry Pi is connected to the Internet via Wifi or Ethernet and is on the same network as your Mac or PC.

The Bare Minimum You Need to Start Playing Games

There's a lot of information in this chapter. Much of it is about fine-tuning the many features of RetroPie. If your main goal is to start playing games, the good news is most of what you need to know was already presented in Chapter 2. As long as you have a controller configured and you know how to install roms, you're good to go. In fact, I recommend that you get

© Mark Frauenfelder and Ryan Bates 2019
M. Frauenfelder and R. Bates, *Raspberry Pi Retro Gaming*,
https://doi.org/10.1007/978-1-4842-5153-9_3

a feel for RetroPie by simply installing roms and playing them for a while. Eventually you'll want to enhance your gaming experience (or will have issues that require information to solve them) and that's what the rest of this chapter, and book, is about.

RetroPie Basics

In this section, we'll get you up to speed on the things you'll need to know to use RetroPie to play different games, save games, and customize the interface. The main configuration menu for RetroPie is in the EmulationStation game carousel (Figure 3-1). Use your controller's D-pad to scroll to the RetroPie icon and press the A button on your controller to activate it (Figure 3-2). This is where you can configure your inputs and outputs and customize other options.

Figure 3-1. *The EmulationStation carousel in RetroPie*

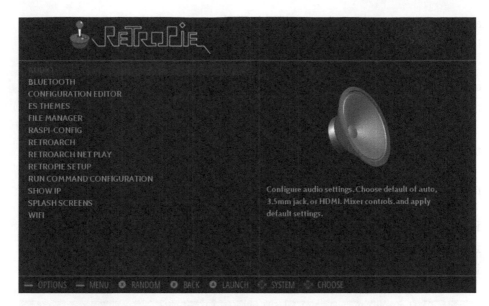

Figure 3-2. *The Raspberry Pi configuration menu*

Caution   Before you make changes to your system, it's a good idea to back up the Pi's microSD card. That way, if you end up making a catastrophic mistake, you won't lose everything. See "How to back up your RetroPie SD Card."

Audio

This menu item lets you select your audio output. Auto will attempt to send the audio to either the HDMI device's speaker or to the Pi's built-in 3.5mm headphone jack. You can also force the output to go through the jack or through the HDMI speakers by selecting the appropriate menu item.

The Mixer menu item lets you set the overall volume.

You'll probably want to be able to adjust the volume of the games you play, as some will be louder than others. The best way to do this (other than connecting a volume knob to the Pi) is to edit your controller's autoconfig file so you can use the Select key and the D-pad's Up and Down controls. Here's how to do it:

Select CONFIGURATION EDITOR from the RetroPie icon in the carousel. Then select Advanced Configuration ➤ Manually edit all configurations.

Use the page down key on your keyboard to scroll down and select all/ retroarch/autoconfig/[controller name].cfg

Scroll to the bottom of the file and enter the following three lines (see Figure 3-3):

```
input_enable_hotkey_btn = 8
input_volume_up_axis = -1
input_volume_down_axis = +1
```

Figure 3-3. *To be able to adjust the volume using your controller, add the three lines at the bottom to your controller configuration file*

Select OK to save the file and then press the Esc key on your keyboard to back out back to the carousel. Then press Start on your controller, select QUIT, then select RESTART EMULATIONSTATION.

Note   These volume controls work on RetroArch/Libretro emulators only. Standalone emulators like the N64 won't be affected. (You can tell if an emulator is supported by Libreto because the filename starts with lr-.)

Bluetooth

This is where you can pair wireless controllers to the Raspberry Pi. Pairing to a Bluetooth controller can be a bit tedious, because it involves some trial and error. Because there are so many different controllers, it's not possible to provide specific instructions for all of them. Here are the general instructions:

Use a wired controller to select BLUETOOTH from the main menu.

Put your wireless controller into discovery mode, then select Register and Connect to Bluetooth Device on the menu. The search could take up to a minute.

One of the discovered devices should say "Gamepad," "Wireless Controller," or something similar. Select it.

You'll then be asked to select a security mode to pair the controller. This is where it gets a bit tricky. There are five different security modes to choose from. Try the first one, and if it doesn't work, try the next one. One of the five options should work.

Select Set up udev rule for joypad and add Gamepad. You'll be asked to reboot. Do this by returning to the EmulationStation carousel, then pressing START, QUIT, and RESTART SYSTEM.

Return to the EmulationStation carousel and press A on your wired controller. Select CONFIGURE INPUT. Confirm that you want to do this by selecting YES, then hold down a button on your wireless controller, and follow the prompts to map the different controls.

Configuration Editor

The Configuration Editor (shown in Figure 3-4) is where you can make tweaks to all the different emulators supported by Libreto (an application program interface (API) for the games and emulators in RetroPie). This is the place where you can configure settings for shading, aspect ratio, smoothing, and scan lines for different emulators.

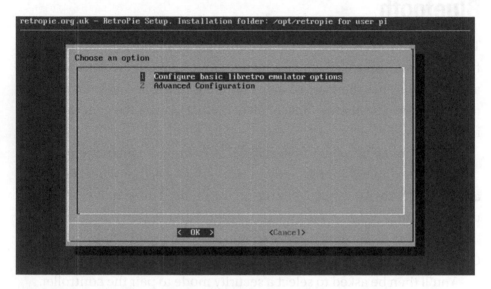

Figure 3-4. *The Configuration Editor menu*

Installing and Using Overlays

Overlays (Figure 3-5) can be used to mimic the actual bezels of different TV sets and handheld players to provide a nostalgic feel to games.

You can apply these changes to all emulators, or just to specific platforms.

Figure 3-5. *An overlay for the Nintendo Game Boy*

RetroPie comes preinstalled with many different shaders, but if you want to use an overlay, you'll have to install it. A quick online search for "retropie overlays" will provide you with a wide variety of overlays. Here's how to install them.

1. Use an SSH file manager like WinSCP or Cyberduck to log into your Pi. (See the File Manager section)

2. Navigate to the folder `/opt/retropie/configs/all/ retroarch/overlay`.

3. Copy the overlay files (there should by a .cfg and a .png for each overlay) into this folder.

4. Once the files have copied, restart EmulationStation on your Pi.

5. Open one of the games you want to apply the overlay to. Once it starts, use the hotkey to open the RetroArch menu. (For the NES controller, the hotkey is Select+X; for other controllers, it could be Select+Y.) Press B to get out of the Quick Menu and get back to the Main Menu.

6. Select Settings ➤ Onscreen Display ➤ Onscreen Overlay ➤ Overlay Preset from the RetroArch menu. Then select the overlay you want by scrolling through the different overlays you just uploaded.

7. Now comes a bit of trial and error. You need to reduce the size of the game display so it fits inside the window of the overlay. Go to Settings ➤ Video ➤ Aspect Ratio. Select Custom. Then use the left and right D-pad controls to adjust the values for the Custom Aspect Ratio X Pos, Custom Aspect Ratio Y Pos, Custom Aspect Ratio X Width, and Custom Aspect Ratio Height. Press Select-X to see how close your window matches up with the overlay, then adjust again until you are satisfied with the result. See Figure 3-5.

8. Press B on your controller until you see Quick Menu. Scroll down to Overrides and select it. If you want to save the overlay to all the games for a certain emulator, then select Save Core Overrides. If you just want to have the overlay apply to the current game, then select Save Game Overrides.

Using Shaders and Scan Lines

Smoothing adds a bit of softness to the graphics by blurring the pixels slightly, while shading (Figure 3-6) gives a slight curvature to the display so that the graphics look as if they're on the curved glass of an old cathode ray tube CRT television set. Scan lines add horizontal stripes to the graphics, to emulate the appearance of a lower-resolution CRT video monitor.

Figure 3-6. *The game on the left has shading and scan line filters applied to it. The image on the right has no filters*

HDMI displays are much crisper and sharper than the CRT displays that were around during the 1970s to early 1990s. Some people like their retro-games to appear as they did on the original equipment—with scan lines, curvature (CRTs have convex screens, which creates a slightly fisheyed image), and blooming (the tendency for lighter-colored pixels to blend into neighboring pixels). If you are one of these people, then you need to use a shader, which is a filter that makes your modern display look like a CRT from decades ago.

To use a shader, start a game and press Select-X on your controller to get to RetroArch's Quick Menu. Scroll down to Shaders and select it. Select Load Shader Preset and you will be presented with many different shader preset files. A popular shader preset is crt-pi-curvature.glslp. You can try that one or any of the other shaders. You can even combine multiple shaders at the same time by highlighting Shader Passes and using D-Pad R to increase the number of shader slots. To get rid of one or more shaders, you can decrement the number of Shader Passes to 0 using D-pad L. Likewise you can use D-Pad L or D-pad R to adjust the Shader Scale, which controls the intensity of the effect. Once you're happy with your shading setup, select Apply Changes. To permanently apply shaders to a game, select Save Game Preset. To apply the shaders to all the games on the emulator, select Save Core Preset.

Tip   What to do if you mess up your RetroArch settings? There are so many different configuration options in RetroPie that you could easily end up with results that look awful. If you've made a bunch of changes and don't remember how to get back to square one, fear not; it's easy to wipe the slate clean and restore the default settings.

Use Cyberduck or WinSCP and navigate to /opt/retropie/ configs/[system name]/

Look for two files in the folder—retroarch.cfg and retroarch. cfg.rp-dist. retroarch.cfg has your current (undesirable) settings, and retroarch.cfg.rp-dist has the default settings for your emulator. Delete retroarch.cfg. Then make a copy of retroarch.cfg.rp-dist and rename it to retroarch.cfg. Restart EmulationStation and you'll be ready to start over.

ES Themes

RetroPie's default interface theme (called Carbon) is perfectly adequate, but there are a large number of attractive interface themes you can install if you want a customized look. There are two main steps: installing a theme and activating it.

To get started with themes, you need to do a couple of preparatory steps. First, press START on your controller and select OTHER SETTINGS ➤ VRAM LIMIT. Use D-pad R to increase the VRAM to 100Mb (this will be enough for most themes). Press B on your controller until you are back in EmulationStation.

Select the RetroPie from the carousel, then select RETROPIE SETUP. Scroll down and select Update RetroPie-Setup script. This will upload a list of the latest themes.

Exit the Setup script menu. Scroll up to ES THEMES and select it with the A button on your controller. You'll see a menu as shown in Figure 3-7. You can now download and install any theme you want to try. Exit the menu.

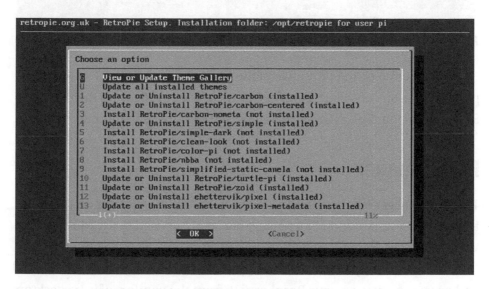

Figure 3-7. *The EmulationStation Themes menu*

Select START on your controller and scroll to THEME SET. Use D-pad L and D-pad R to choose the theme you want to activate. Here's what the Pixel theme looks like (Figure 3-8).

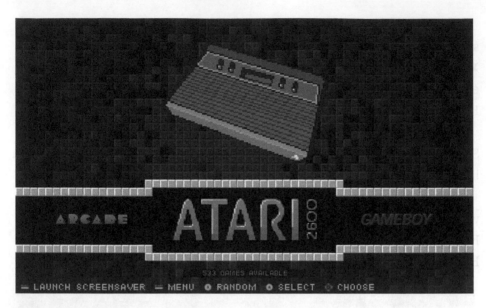

Figure 3-8. *The Pixel theme*

You can also change the style of the transitions between platforms—you can select from Instant, Fade, or Slide from the UI SETTINGS menu. Try all three styles and see which one you prefer.

File Manager

The file manager is for copying, moving, and deleting the files on the Pi's microSD card. I don't like using it because I'm used to my Mac and Windows interfaces with their convenient click-and-drag functionality.

There are a couple of great free apps that make it easy for you to upload and access the files on your Raspberry Pi from the comfort of your desktop or laptop computer: WinSCP (https://winscp.net/) for Windows and Cyberduck (https://cyberduck.io/) for Mac.

Once you install the programs, you can connect to the Pi by entering its IP address (see in Chapter 2 to find out what your Pi's IP address is) and the username and password for your Pi (the default username is pi and the default password is raspberry). Make sure to specify an SFTP or SSH connection, as shown in Figure 3-9.

Figure 3-9. *Using Cyberduck to connect to your Raspberry Pi from a Mac computer*

With Cyberduck or WinSCP running on your computer, it's a snap to manage files on your Pi. These programs also make it easy to move files between your Pi and your computer. You can also edit configuration files on your Pi using your favorite text editor (mine is BBEdit, which is much easier than using a Linux text editor like nano).

Raspi-Config

This menu item is discussed in Chapter 2.

RetroArch

The basic functions of RetroArch are covered separately throughout this chapter.

RetroArch Net Play

You can play games online with other people around the world through Netplay. Refer to the menu in Figure 3-10. At the top you will see your Internal IP and External IP. I scribbled out my External IP in the example earlier because it could be used by hackers to infiltrate my home network. However, the External IP is what you need to share with a friend if you are running the game as a Host. If you are running as a client, your friend will have to give you their External IP and port, which you'll enter in menu items 2 and 3. You can create a nickname by selecting menu item 4. Save with menu item 5.

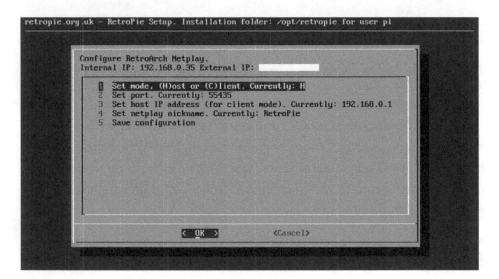

Figure 3-10.   *Setting up RetroPie for Netplay*

Not all emulators can be used for Netplay, and some are glitchier than others; you'll just have to try them and see what works. Importantly, you and your friend will need to have the exact same game rom and emulator (also known as a core) versions as well as the same version of Retroarch to be able to play against each other.

Once you've got all this set up, you can tell your friend to start a game. When you start the same game, press a key on your controller to bring up the game's configuration menu, and scroll down to Launch with netplay enabled.

RetroPie Setup

This menu item is for installing the latest version of RetroPie, installing extra and experimental packages, and configuring the software. The RetroPie Setup menu is shown in Figure 3-11.

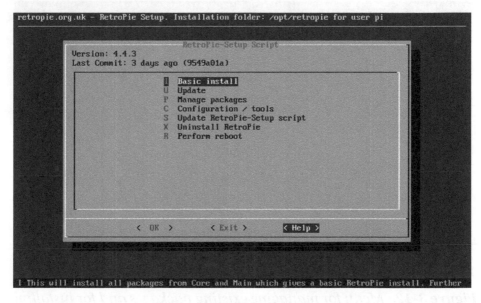

Figure 3-11. *The RetroPie Setup menu*

Basic Install

This installs the latest version of RetroPie and its basic components, such as RetroArch, EmulationStation, and standalone emulators. This operation takes up to 10 minutes to complete. Since you already have RetroPie running, you don't need to install it.

Update

This menu item updates all the packages you've installed and the RetroPie-Setup script.

Manage Packages

If you want to update emulators or controller drivers individually, or install ones that aren't included in the basic package, use this menu item, shown in Figure 3-12.

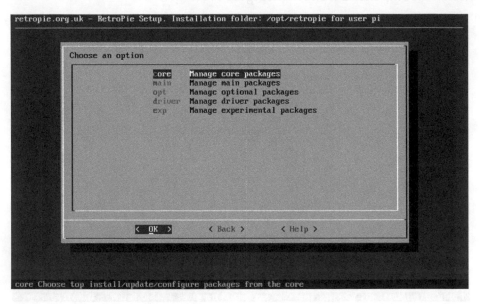

Figure 3-12. *Menu for managing existing packages and for installing experimental and new packages*

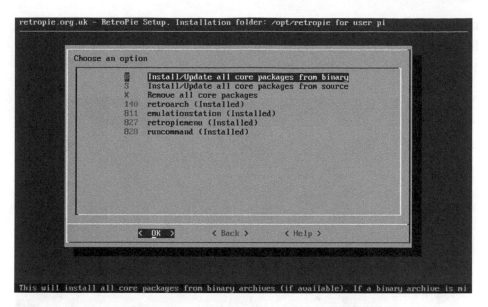

Figure 3-13. *Options to install/update RetroPie emulator cores*

Manage Core Packages

This menu lets you update core components of RetroPie: RetroArch, EmulationStation, the RetroPie Menu, and Run Command. If, for some reason, you need to update one or more of these components, it's better to install them from binary instead of source, because source could involve debugging with Linux commands. (If you're a Linux wizard, have at it!)

Manage Main Packages

This is where you can update the emulators that came pre-installed with RetroPie. Again, it's better to install from the binary rather than source.

Manage Optional Packages

There are many emulators available that don't come preinstalled on RetroPie. This is the place to install them. As you can see in Figure 3-14, I've installed DOSBox so I can play games that run on IBM-compatible

73

computers running the DOS operating system. This menu item also lets you install some shareware versions of games, like *Quake 3 and Wolfenstein 3D*, as well as an alternate scraper.

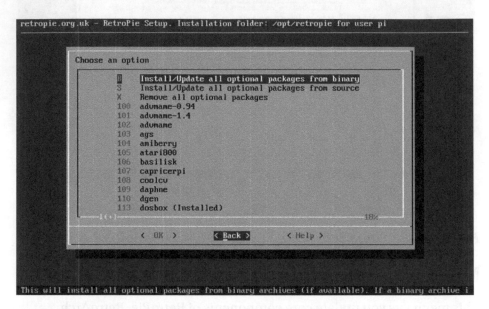

Figure 3-14. *The Manage Optional Packages menu*

Manage Driver Packages

This is where you can install drivers for controllers not included in RetroPie, like the one for the PS3 or Xbox. See Figure 3-15.

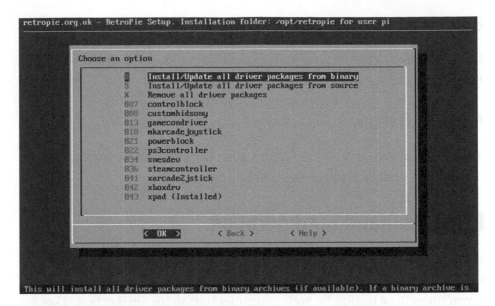

Figure 3-15. *The Manage drivers packages menu*

Manage Experimental Packages

The emulators, control drivers, and games here haven't been thoroughly tested with RetroPie and may have bugs and other issues.

Configuration/Tools

You can configure Bluetooth and Wifi setting here, as well as themes and splashscreens. Most of the options in this menu are covered elsewhere in the book when the need to use them arises.

Update RetroPie-Setup Script

This updates the setup script to the latest version. It's a good idea to run this before doing anything in this section.

Uninstall RetroPie

If you installed RetroPie on top of another Linux OS, this will remove
RetroPie while keeping everything else intact.

Perform Reboot

Yet another way to reboot the Pi. It's a good idea to reboot your system
once you're done making changes in RetroPie Setup.

Run Command Configuration

When you launch a game, you'll notice a small window appears before
the game actually starts running. It's called the Runcommand Launch menu.
If you press the A button on your controller button (or any keyboard key)
before the game launches, you can configure various settings for the game,
such as the emulator, video mode, the RetroArch configuration, and so
on. You can set up the behavior of the Runcommand Launch menu from this
menu item (Figure 3-16).

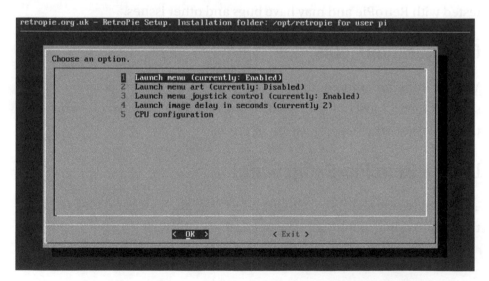

Figure 3-16. *The Run Command Configuration menu*

If you don't want to see the Runcommand Launch menu every time you start a game, highlight Launch menu and press A, and the status will be set to Disabled.

You can also make the Launch menu look cool using the second menu item, Launch menu art. You can use any .jpg or .png image you want. Name the image launching.png or launching.jpg and copy it to the appropriate folder using Cyberduck or WinSCP. See Figure 3-17 for an example.

Here's a source for some nice-looking launching images: https://github.com/ehettervik/es-runcommand-splash. Unzip the file, and copy over each launching.png file you want to use to /opt/retropie/configs/[system name]/

Figure 3-17. *Launching.png file for the Game Boy Color, created by hettervik*

Launch menu joystick control allows you to enable or disable the ability to call the Runcommand Launch menu from a joystick. (You'll still be able to use your keyboard to access the menu.)

Launch Image Delay lets you specify how many seconds to display launching.png before the game loads.

CPU configuration is used to change the way the Raspberry Pi's CPU behaves under certain conditions. You probably don't need to change the default setting unless you are overclocking your Pi to run a Nintendo 64 emulator, in which case you should select Force performance. Don't use this setting unless you have a fan blowing air on the Pi's CPU.

Show IP

This menu item shows the network IP address of your Raspberry Pi. See Figure 3-18 for an example. You'll need this to remotely connect to the Pi from a Mac or PC.

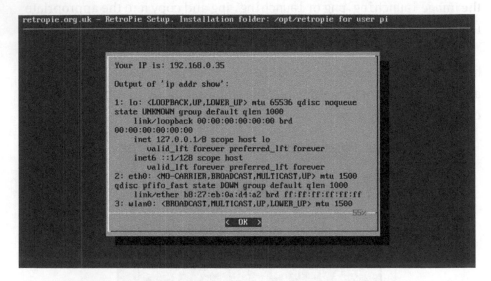

Figure 3-18. *The Show IP screen. In this case, the IP address of the Pi is 192.168.0.35*

Splash Screens

When you start up your Pi, it displays a default splash screen image of the RetroPie logo. You can change it to any image you want or even play a video. Your options here are shown in Figure 3-19, and described in the following list:

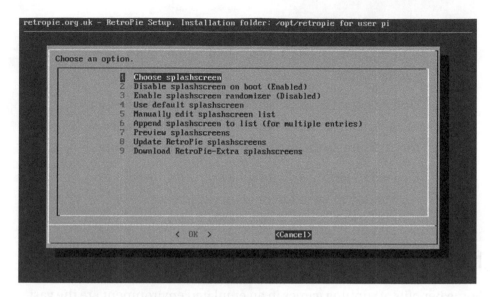

Figure 3-19. *The Splash Screen menu*

- Choose splashscreen. RetroPie comes installed with several different splash screen options. You can select one here. If you've added additional splash screen files, you can also select them from this menu item.

- Disable splashscreen on boot. If you don't want a splash screen when you start up the Pi, use this menu item.

- Enable splashscreen randomizer. This allows you to choose from several different ways to display a random splash screen every time you start up the Pi.

- Use default splashscreen. This resets to the default splash screen.

- Manually edit splashscreen list. It isn't convenient to edit the list of splash screens using this menu item. It's much easier to use Cyberduck or WinSCP, navigate to /etc/splashscreen.list and edit the file with a text editor.

79

- Append splashscreen to list. See earlier items.

- Preview splashscreens. Take a look at the images before you select one.

- Update RetroPie splashscreens. If changes have been made to splash screens you've already downloaded, this will refresh the directory with the latest versions.

- Download RetroPie-Extra splashscreens. Use this menu item to download additional splash screens.

Helpful Information

Some benefits of running games in an emulated environment are the vast customization options we've discussed previously along with the ability to "save" or freeze your game anywhere during gameplay. Undoubtedly you may have invested significant time tweaking settings just to your preference and sunk many hours into a game that doesn't have integratedsave game features. The next few topics will cover how to back up your RetroArch customizations, game saves, and all contents on your SD card.

Backing Up Your RetroPie SD Card

Just as it's smart to regularly back up your Mac or PC hard drive, you should back up your Pi's microSD card, especially before you change configuration settings. The easiest way to back up the microSD card is to make a full image from it. The procedure is different depending on whether you're using a Mac or a PC.

Backing Up on a Mac

Shut down the Pi and remove the microSD card. Put it in an adaptor or a USB reader and plug it into your Mac. Open a Terminal window and enter diskutil list. This will show you all the storage devices connected to your system. Look for a device that has the same memory capacity as your microSD card (it will be smaller than your hard drive) and take note of the disk number. In Figure 3-20, you can see that my microSD card is 8.0 GB and is disk2. (It's important to correctly identify the disk number; otherwise, you will end up making a copy of one of your other disks.)

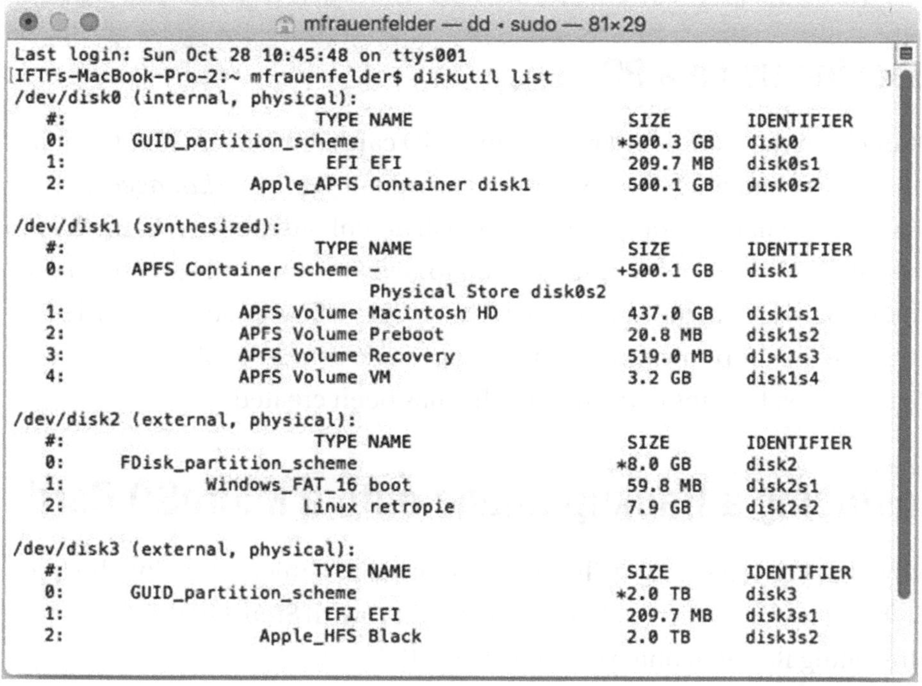

```
● ● ●                    mfrauenfelder — dd · sudo — 81×29
Last login: Sun Oct 28 10:45:48 on ttys001
[IFTFs-MacBook-Pro-2:~ mfrauenfelder$ diskutil list
/dev/disk0 (internal, physical):
   #:                       TYPE NAME                    SIZE       IDENTIFIER
   0:      GUID_partition_scheme                        *500.3 GB   disk0
   1:                        EFI EFI                     209.7 MB   disk0s1
   2:                 Apple_APFS Container disk1         500.1 GB   disk0s2

/dev/disk1 (synthesized):
   #:                       TYPE NAME                    SIZE       IDENTIFIER
   0:       APFS Container Scheme -                      +500.1 GB  disk1
                                  Physical Store disk0s2
   1:                APFS Volume Macintosh HD            437.0 GB   disk1s1
   2:                APFS Volume Preboot                 20.8 MB    disk1s2
   3:                APFS Volume Recovery                519.0 MB   disk1s3
   4:                APFS Volume VM                      3.2 GB     disk1s4

/dev/disk2 (external, physical):
   #:                       TYPE NAME                    SIZE       IDENTIFIER
   0:      FDisk_partition_scheme                       *8.0 GB     disk2
   1:             Windows_FAT_16 boot                    59.8 MB    disk2s1
   2:                      Linux retropie                7.9 GB     disk2s2

/dev/disk3 (external, physical):
   #:                       TYPE NAME                    SIZE       IDENTIFIER
   0:      GUID_partition_scheme                        *2.0 TB     disk3
   1:                        EFI EFI                     209.7 MB   disk3s1
   2:                  Apple_HFS Black                   2.0 TB     disk3s2
```

Figure 3-20. *Results of entering* diskutil *list into Mac's Terminal window. Note that the microSD card is* disk2

Enter the following command in the Terminal window:

```
sudo dd if=/dev/[disk#] of=~/Desktop/retropie.dmg
```

In my case [disk#] is disk2. Also, you can name the file something other than retropie.dmg if you wish. You'll probably be asked to enter your password. (This is the password of your Mac account, not your Pi.) When you enter it and press Return, you won't see any activity in the Terminal window. It will appear as though nothing is happening. Just be patient. An 8GB microSD card could take up to a half hour to download.

Once it's finished, your file will have a .dmg extension. You'll need to edit the file name to say .img if you want to install it on a microSD card.

Backing Up on a PC

Shut down the Pi and remove the microSD card. Put it in an adaptor or a USB reader and plug it into your PC. Download *Win32DiskImager* from Sourceforge.net. (It's only 12MB, so it will download quickly.) Launch it. In the Image File field, enter the location to save the image file and the name you want to give it, for example, C:/Users/Mark/Downloads/retropie. img. Use the dropdown menu for the Device to select the SD card. Click Read. You will be notified when the file has been created.

Installing a Backup Image onto a MicroSD Card

Now that you have a .img file, you can burn it to a microSD using the free Etcher utility, as described in Chapter 2. Start with Step 4 in the section "Installing RetroPie onto your Raspberry Pi."

Tip   It's a good idea to reformat an SD card before you install an image to it. Download a free formatter from www.sdcard.org/downloads/formatter_4/.

Installing Roms

Refer to ("Installing a game on RetroPie"), which shows you two ways to get roms installed in RetroPie.

Scraping

Do you want to see cover art and descriptions of your installed games? If so, then you need a scraper. This is a software utility that scours the Internet for art and game descriptions so you can display them in the EmulationStation carousel. RetroPie includes a built-in scraping utility, but most people swear by a utility called Skyscraper, which is available at `https://github.com/muldjord/skyscraper`.

To install it, you can either use SSH to connect to your Raspberry Pi via your desktop or laptop or you can connect a keyboard to your Pi, quit EmulationStation (see section "Shutting Down Your Pi, Rebooting, or Quitting EmulationStation"), and enter the following commands:

```
sudo apt-get update

sudo apt-get install qt5-default

cd

mkdir skysource

cd skysource

wget -q -O - https://raw.githubusercontent.com/muldjord/
skyscraper/master/update_skyscraper.sh | bash
```

It will take several minutes for the final command to complete. Once you see the command prompt again, simply enter Skyscraper. You'll be presented with some introductory text as seen in Figure 3-21 and then asked a series of questions.

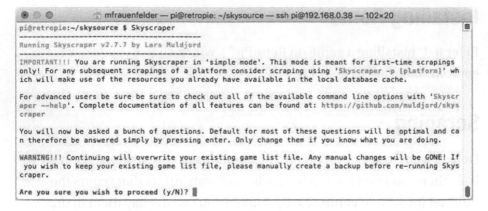

Figure 3-21. *The Skyscraper utility*

For most questions, you should press the Enter key to provide the default answer.

When you're done answering them, Skyscraper will generate a script and ask you if you are ready to execute it. Press Enter or Y to proceed.

After the script runs, you can rerun Skyscraper and specify another game platform for it to scrape. Repeat until all of your platforms have been scraped, then restart EmulationStation (if you're working on the Pi, enter EmulationStation; if you are working on a computer using SSH to access the Pi, use the controller connected to the Pi and follow the instructions in the section "How to Shut Down Your Pi, Reboot, or Quit EmulationStation").

Now, when you look at the list of games in your carousel, you'll see cover art and a game description, as in Figure 3-22.

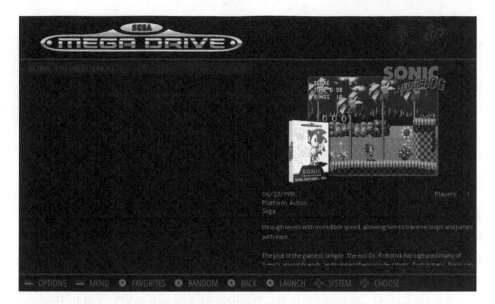

Figure 3-22. *Scraping adds useful game information to your EmulationStation games carousel*

Note   Skyscraper has a number of features for customization. To see them, enter `Skyscraper -help`

Leaving a Game

To stop playing a game and return the emulation carousel, press `start+select`. Press B to load the emulator carousel. If you want to save your game progress before leaving a game, the next section will show you how.

Saving Game States

When you play a game on a console or your computer, it's easy to save your progress in a game. But it's not so straightforward when you use RetroPie.

If you simply quit out of the game by pressing select+start your progress won't be saved. Fortunately, RetroPie has a function that allows you to save the state of your game so you can leave and return at the same place you left off. The cool thing about the RetroPie's save state function is that you can save your progress at any point, not just at milestone points.

To save a game at any point, press select + right shoulder button on your gamepad. If you want to load the save state, press select + left shoulder button.

You can also save game states to as many different slots as you want. The default slot is zero. To increment the slot number, press select + D-pad right. To decrement the slot number, press select + D-pad left. Then to save in that slot, press select + right shoulder button. To load, press select + left shoulder button.

The save slots are stored on the Raspberry Pi's microSD card in the roms folder.

Shutting Down Your Pi, Rebooting, or Quitting EmulationStation

Avoid shutting off your Raspberry Pi simply by removing the power cord. This will leave a bunch of Linux processes hanging and could corrupt data or even cause physical damage to the microSD card. Instead, enter a shutdown command. To do this in RetroPie, press Start, and scroll down to QUIT in the menu. You'll be given four options:

RESTART EMULATIONSTATION
QUIT EMULATIONSTATION
RESTART SYSTEM
SHUTDOWN SYSTEM

Use RESTART EMULATIONSTATION after you've installed a rom or theme, or have customized the system. This simply quits EmulationStation and restarts it.

QUIT EMULATIONSTATION will quit the program and present you with the Linux command line. (To restart EmulationStation from the command line, enter emulationstation on the keyboard.)

RESTART SYSTEM fully reboots the Pi. If you have an SSH or server connection to the Pi from another computer, the connection will be terminated, and you'll have to log in again.

SHUTDOWN SYSTEM is the command to use when you want to power down the Pi. Once you enter the command, you'll see a bunch of text scroll by on the screen. But don't unplug the power source just yet. Wait about 20 seconds to allow Linux to execute its various housekeeping tasks first. If you don't have your Pi in a case, you can keep your eye on the little green LED—after it blinks 10 times, you can cut the power.

Summary

We've explored many features and customization options to tweak your RetroPie experience. Some are simple aesthetic changes like custom borders that play homage to your favorite handheld, while others are true quality-of-life improvements like adding the ability to save your game at any time regardless of its hardware origins. We touched base on the deep inner workings of the RetroPie core, to keep it current and with newer builds and version released as well as know how to back up your efforts spent customizing the software well. Speaking of, the aforementioned customizations were all done in software. If you want not just the look but also the feel of long-lost gaming memories, read on. Next, we will start to explore custom hardware options to complete the experience.

CHAPTER 4

Enclosure for Your Raspberry Pi

First thing on your wish list after setting up the Raspberry Pi (RPi) is an enclosure. Something to protect it from the elements and christen it with the proper respect of a "game console." In this chapter, I'll start with some of the most bare-bone, no-frills enclosures. Fortunately, most of these are readily available shells and cases you can purchase from vendors on amazon.com, Adafruit.com, eBay.com, and (to circumvent reseller markups) alibaba.com or aliexpress.com. I have to warn you, there are a lot of options available. The educated buyer is least likely to feel buyer's remorse. The following enclosures range from merely covering your Pi's naked PCB to adding some thermal management and even dressing up the Pi to look like an old retro game console.

Common Enclosures

The most common case you'll find is a bare-minimum, two-piece enclosure that snaps together. This is the most abundant case in the wild, especially on Amazon and eBay. I'm just pulling one example that ranks in the "okay" quality range. In this bottom-tier range, expect to pay more in shipping than the cost of actual case. In hindsight, you'll wish you bought these at checkout with your Raspberry Pi. The cases shown in Figures 4-1

© Mark Frauenfelder and Ryan Bates 2019
M. Frauenfelder and R. Bates, *Raspberry Pi Retro Gaming*,
https://doi.org/10.1007/978-1-4842-5153-9_4

through 4-3 are likely what you get if you just pick the first piece of plastic in a Google search of "Raspberry Pi case." This vast selection of mediocrity lies within a general price range of $2–$8, depending on how frugal you search for a nickel's worth of injection molded plastic. This is by no means an indication of the quality of the case, some are rather good. The mold is usually accurate to the Pi's dimensions, and decent plastic is used in the mold.

Figure 4-1. *Plain Black Cases for Raspberry Pi*

Most of these cases are snap fit and usually do nothing more than dress up your RPi level above a bare circuit board. Depending on your mileage and applications for the future, cases with cutouts that allow access the GPIOs, camera, and display ZIF connectors might be a feature worth having.

Figure 4-2. *Raspberry Pi resting in the lower half of a generic plastic case*

Figure 4-3. *Raspberry Pi resting snugly in a case*

While there is nothing inherently wrong with these cases, do read on. Some of these cases take on some unusual design aesthetics to stand out from other two-piece cases and in the process have some design flaws. These flaws can be rather deal breaking like interfering with USB or HDMI cables with bulky shrouds on the cable end. You're more likely to toss that $4 case then buy a new HDMI cable. You'll likely avoid a case of buyer remorse if you take some time to see all your options for Raspberry Pi cases. These simple plastic cases are more for the hardware hacker that just needs to protect their integrated Pi within their larger hardware project. You can do a lot better to show off the work put into your retro game console enclosure if you continue your search efforts.

The Official Solution

Recently the Raspberry Pi Foundation officially released their own case. This case should only be purchased from verified resellers listed on the Raspberrypi.org web site. This case is likely the most copied case as it closely associates the reputation of the Raspberry Pi with a branded logo on top. This case, shown in the figure, is solely a snap fit case. No additional hardware is required. The official Raspberry Pi case makes a quality case that requires no setup time if you simply want to protect your Raspberry Pi and move one.

Figure 4-4 shows the official Raspberry Pi case; note the branded Raspberry Pi logo.

Figure 4-4. *Official Raspberry Pi case*

A nice feature of this enclosure is its modularity as shown in Figures 4-5 and 4-6. Need to access the GPIOs? Simply remove the top snap fit panel. Have a bulky HDMI cable that just will not make full electrical contract? Remove the A/V header panel.

Figure 4-5. *Disassembled Official Raspberry Pi case*

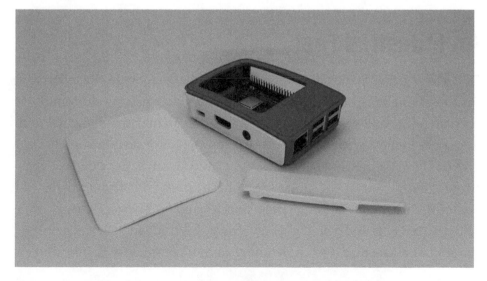

Figure 4-6. *Partially assembled Official Raspberry Pi case*

All the panels are snap fit (think Tupperware), making this an impressive case that retails (at the time of this writing) around $7. Again, this case carries a branded name; therefore it is also the most susceptible to knockoffs and counterfeits. The mold requires some precision to make a robust snap fit, and this is likely the first compromise you'll notice if you unknowingly purchase a counterfeit case. The Raspberry Pi Foundation lists these US sites as authorized resellers of the Official Raspberry Pi case:

- Chicago Electronic Distributors

- Pi Shop.us

- CanaKit

- Micro Center

This list expands for other countries, so be sure to visit `www.raspberrypi.org/products/raspberry-pi-a-case/` for authorized resellers in your area.

If you like the reputation the RPi carries and prefer a simple, it-just-fits case to protect the RPi, look no further. This case is also produced in black/gray if the red/white color theme doesn't suit your taste.

An Industrial Feel

"If it's heavy, then it must be expensive" is also a category for Raspberry Pi cases. From what started as a solid block of metal, usually aluminum, you can encapsulate your Pi in the fine finishing of machined metal. From anywhere in the low range of $15 to $50 and up, these cases definitely give the Pi some heft and beef. An appreciated factor is the added weight. If your gold-plated HDMI cable pulls your Raspberry Pi off your media center shelf, a metal case might help affix it in place. These cases are also a mixed bag, and going off of reviews is one thing to help weed out the subpar enclosures. CNC machining cannot complete with injection molding economies of scale, so if you see a "CNC machined" case in the same price range as an injection molded case, I would stay away.

Figures 4-7 and 4-8 show a low-range metal case (found on amazon. com for around $15) made from aluminum. Fortunately, the Raspberry Pi's mechanical footprint has been pretty consistent since the Pi 2 B+ model; therefore injection molded cases have come down significantly since the tooling has paid for itself. Assuming the Pi footprint will not change, production CNC machining can closer match the plastic molded price range over time. Prices for machined cases have dropped since their first appearance in the market. Just note, if you are seeking a purely machined case, you will be paying for the machine and tooling time. There are little economies of scale when every case must be machined from a solid block of metal. Expect to pay for the premium cases. I can tell you I did not buy one just to take a photo of it.

Figure 4-7. *Aluminum-molded Raspberry Pi case, topside*

One nice feature about solid metal cases is the heat dissipation method, likely passive in the following example. If you find a well-toleranced case, some include a protrusion of metal. This protrusion is usually positioned right above the Pi's main processor, and with some thermal tape to bridge the very tiny gap, the case is now the CPU heatsink. The case pulls heat from the CPU with the help of thermally conductive tape or foam to transfer heat from the Pi's main CPU to the case.

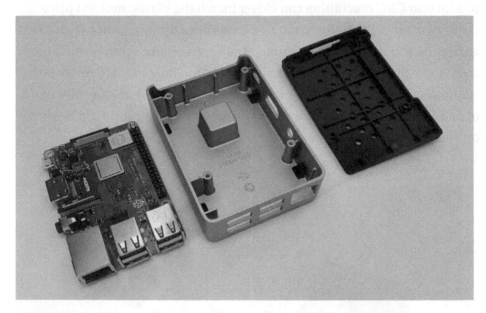

Figure 4-8. *Aluminum-molded Raspberry Pi case, underside*

With the help of some thermally conductive paste or tape, you can remove (sink) heat generated from the Pi's main processor and dissipate this heat into the case itself. Again, this feature requires dimensions with relatively tight tolerances, and if the price of your case seems just too good, don't expect this claim to ring true. If you look closely at Figure 4-8, you can see tooling remnants (a small ring left from the tool mold) at the contact point of the heatsink to CPU junction. This protrusion should ideally be machined smooth. You will get what you pay for.

3D Printed Case

Continuing with a DIY theme, 3D printed cases are the most prevalent in design and low-cost options (if you own a 3D printer). Ranging in the simplest designs to ones that tailor to a specific theme or icon of gaming. If you've ventured in the realm of 3D printing, you've probably already looked at thingiverse.com for user submitted designs. The following case (Figure 4-9) was printed from user Walter Hsiao on thingiverse.com under the search name "Sleeve case for Raspberry Pi." This is a two-piece case, but just the larger part will suffice to protect your RPi.

Figure 4-9. *Sleeve Vase for Raspberry Pi by walter*

3D printed cases can be temperamental depending on the printer you use. Everyone designs using a slightly different process, so unless you have a finely tuned and well-calibrated printer, the case you print might be too small by a fraction of a millimeter and you'll find yourself running another 12-hour print. The highest rated or most popular submissions on thingiverse.com are usually quite reliable and viable options. I don't recommend the 3D printed enclosure route unless you own a printer. Reprinting because of user error is rite of passage with 3D printers.

One must embrace the process of reprinting parts because you forgot to account for part shrinkage. But if 3D printing feels more like a hassle, there are other options.

Of course, there are online printing services, but it really defeats the appeal of 3D printing—producing a part on the spot. If you're fortunate to own or have access to a 3D printer, thingiverse.com is a great resource.

Thinking Out of the Box

I can say one feature you will find in abundance with Raspberry Pi cases on Thingiverse is many case options including a rear-TV mount method. If you make a case for your Pi, you still have to figure out where to put this tiny box among your other substantially larger media equipment. The simplest way to address the "where to put my Pi" among your gaming setup is to sidestep the problem. Just hide it. Why not mount the Pi behind your TV or monitor? Here's a take on mounting a Raspberry Pi to an LCD monitor in Figures 4-10 and 4-11.

Figure 4-10. *Rear mount VESA bracket on a 19" monitor*

The TV mount is a handy feature if your TV is freestanding and you'd rather have the RPi tucked out of the way. The method I demonstrated is for smaller monitors (19" pictured).

Figure 4-11. *Closer look at rear-mount VESA bracket*

I use this as a cheap, all-in-one computer for teaching or tabling at conventions. The carry handle is the key feature. If your TV or monitor has a built-in power connection like 12VDC on many business class Dell monitors, you could tap into this and power your Pi. That's what I've done in Figure 4-12. Pictured is an overengineered step-down converter PCB with the same mounting pattern as the RPi. Threaded standoffs keep everything connected to the VESA bracket.

Figure 4-12. *Buck converter mounted on Pi*

Rear mounting your Pi to a TV can be as elegant or as overengineered as you like. Here's a mechanical drawing in Figure 4-13 of the aforementioned method; just add holes to mount your RPi. Note there are a total of four sets of VESA mounting holes: two for 75mm and two for 100mm, all with M4 holes.

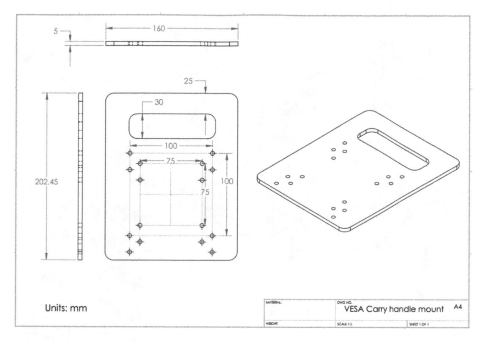

Figure 4-13. *VEA mount details*

You can laser cut this part or just transfer the hole locations to a ¼"-thick piece of wood and be done with it. Strapped to the rear of your TV or monitor, you don't have to worry about the Pi being tugged off your shelf because of heavy HDMI cables or when your cat walks behind your media center.

Themed Cases

As you browse user-submitted content for DIY cases, you'll start to notice many fit a theme. Some satisfy specific tastes like Han Solo frozen in carbonite shown in Figure 4-14.

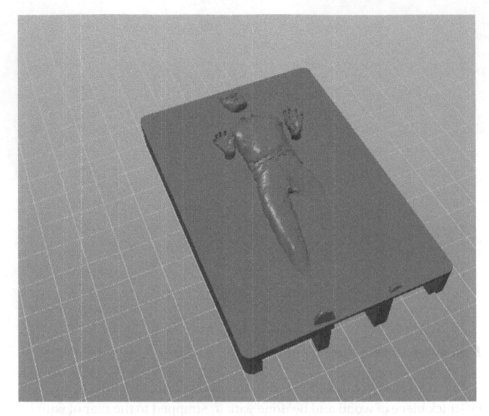

Figure 4-14. *Han Solo in Carbonite 3D printed case by*
TheAtomicSoul

Along these same lines, one can find more refined tastes among the
retro gaming themes. Printing a NES, Sega Genesis, SNES, or PlayStation
style console is pretty common; however, there are better options.
Manufacturers spend time looking for trends via video game themes.
Raspberry Pi cases are no different. The retro gaming market is in a bit of
a renaissance in more than just HD remasters. In regard to Raspberry Pi
cases, the company RetroFlag has produced some exceptional products.
These cases are usually sold on Amazon, through RetroFlag's Amazon
shop, and I strongly suggest you purchase from there, a known source.
There are many imitators of this case. Stick to RetroFlag if you want quality.

Granted this case is nothing more than a glorified USB 2.0 hub, it's the look of a mini NES (that's the North American–style Nintendo Famicom), SNES, or Sega Genesis (Mega Drive in Europe) that makes this case so appealing like the one shown in Figure 4-15.

Figure 4-15.   *RetroFlag Genesis and NES cases*

This is the answer to that nostalgia-driven impulse. These cases retail around $25 and are simple to assemble. The retail packaging (not pictured) alone attests to the care and detail put into the case. Along with the necessary screws to assemble the case, also included is a small screwdriver. It's the attention to detail that pushes this case above standard products in the same category. Let's have a closer look inside the NES case in Figure 4-16.

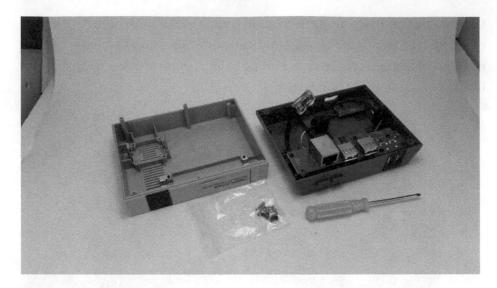

Figure 4-16. *NES case halves*

The Raspberry Pi is mounted per the instructional diagram included with your case. Follow these instructions carefully. The Ethernet extension and USB hub cable are only as long as they need to be and might require some finessing to seat the Pi properly in the case. These cases include room to add a small fan for active cooling, but using a fan to actively cool your Pi is not a must for most emulation tasks. Close the case and secure the remaining screws. The front USB panels shown on the NES case are two additional ports for USB controllers (Figure 4-17).

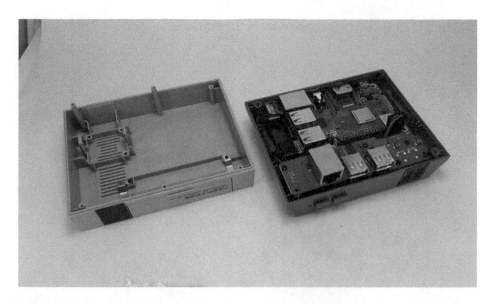

Figure 4-17. *RetroFlag NES case with Pi3 Installed*

Lifting the cartridge cover reveals the Pi's USB and Ethernet connections (Figure 4-18).

Figure 4-18. *RetroFlag NES case lid open*

The SD card can be accessed from the outside as seen in Figure 4-19.

Figure 4-19. *SD card port side of RetroFlag NES case*

RetroFlag even went to the lengths to include a fake expansion port cover that can hide extra microSD cards (Figure 4-20).

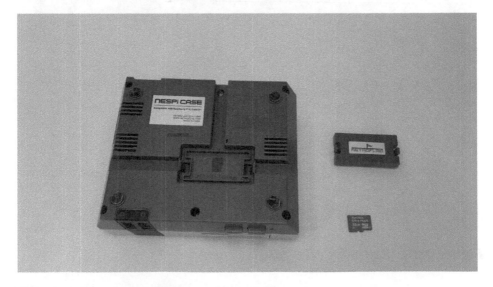

Figure 4-20. *Bottom of RetroFlag NES case*

The outstanding features of this case are the features that extend above just a well-designed enclosure; these are working power and reset buttons (refer to Figure 4-18). Yes, these are functioning buttons. Caution should be known as these are hardwired power-interrupt buttons. Toggling the power or reset buttons will interrupt the main power to your Pi. The buttons on this NES case are not software-enabled buttons that would activate a script and turn off the Pi by activating a shutdown state. These are hard on/off and reset buttons. New versions of these cases add the option to connect to the Pi's GPIOs. Along with some added scripts the user must install, these buttons can be used as soft rest and power buttons. Adjacent to the power button is an illuminated LED. Shown in Figure 4-21 are the final touches of these case designs. The NES case (pictured right) has an access door akin to the front-loading design of the original, while the Genesis case has a hinged top lid for storing SD cards. The latter is not all that useful, but it's still a feature! This probably checks off the final boxes for nostalgia if you're looking for a retro gaming–themed case. I'm more partial to a Sega Genesis, so let's assemble a Mega Drive/Genesis version case from the same manufacturer.

Figure 4-21. *RetroFlag Genesis and NES case with lids open*

Let's start with an unboxing of the case. We can see the included screwdriver and hardware to secure the two halves of the enclosure in Figure 4-22.

Figure 4-22. *RetroFlag Genesis case halves*

Power to the case gets routed from the stand-alone micro USB port in the back. The power port gets rerouted to the PI's 5V and GND GPIO headers shown in Figure 4-23. Be sure to connect this cable with the correct orientation, the wrong way may damage your Pi. This cable is very short, do not pull it.

Figure 4-23. *RetroFlag Genesis with a Pi 3 B+*

Turn the Raspberry Pi upside down, this is how it will rest in the case (Figure 4-24).

Figure 4-24. *Pi turned upside down in RetroFlag Genesis case*

Secure the Pi using the included screws, but only fasten the two holes nearest to the larger PCB within the case (Figure 4-25).

Figure 4-25. *RetroFlag Genesis with Pi 3, interior screw location*

Insert case's USB plug into the Raspberry Pi USB ports (Figures 4-26 and 4-27).

Figure 4-26. *RetroFlag Genesis case USB hub connection*

Figure 4-27. *RetroFlag Genesis case USB hub connection complete*

Place the other half of the enclosure to complete the shell; add five screws to the unused side of the case (near the perimeter) as shown in Figure 4-28.

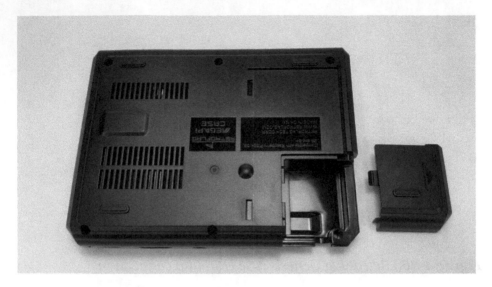

Figure 4-28. *Ethernet access port*

If you need wired Ethernet, you can access the Pi's Ethernet port by removing the panel also shown in Figure 4-28 and route your network cable through this.

The SD card port can be accessed by lifting the side port shown in Figure 4-29.

Figure 4-29. *SD card slot on RetroFlag Genesis case*

Extra SD cards can be stored in the top lid previously shown in Figure 4-21. This RetroFlag Genesis case features something different than the NES case, it has a software shutdown feature that can be implemented with an additional python script. Since the GPIOs 2,3,4, and 15 are wired into reset and power buttons within this case, we can use as labeled but following the Pi's guidelines for safe shutdown and reset. Following the github link included in the instructions (omitted here) will provide details how to install this extra script. This will allow the Raspberry Pi to soft-shutdown or reset via software if the appropriate power or reset button is pressed.

Build Your Own

Outside the realm of designing, laser cutting, or 3D printing a custom case, you can go one step further and pay homage to the console of your choice. Replacement console shells are no longer a common commodity found on eBay, so I recommend (in the respect of preservation of retro game consoles) find an unrepairable console and gut it. In the following example, we will use a PlayStation 1 console with a failed CD-ROM assembly, salvage its shell, and repurpose it as a Raspberry Pi enclosure.

Gathering Supplies

Depending on how detailed you want to get, this can be a very involved process compared to what we've covered previously in this chapter. Let's start by looking at the items needed to build an enclosure with shell from a PlayStation 1 console.

To build the following, you'll need:

- PlayStation 1 model SCPH-1001 (that powers on)
- 3D printer or access to one
- Gray spray paint
- 4x M3x17mm SCPH-1001 standoffs
- 8x M3x8mm screws
- PlayStation 1,2, 3 AC power cable
- Multimeter (to measure voltage)
- 2x USB 3.0 extension cable, 6 inch long
- DC-DC step-down (buck) converter
- Soldering iron
- Misc wires (22–26 AWG) and some heat shrink tubing

Here's a SCPH-1001 model PlayStation, one that will not read discs (Figure 4-30).

Figure 4-30. *SCPH-1001 model PlayStation 1. Very classic*

I've picked an original PlayStation for a few reasons: it has a roomy interior, a large open cutout at the rear (on this particular model shown in Figure 4-31), a power supply, and a switch we can reuse.

Figure 4-31. *Rear view of SCPH-1001 model PlayStation 1. This is the last time we will see nonproprietary AV connections until the HDMI era*

The outer shell is in decent condition. Most indie retro game stores will have a pile of broken consoles in the back deemed not fit for resale. Don't be afraid to ask to take some off their hands. You might get questioned, but as long as you're upfront and not directly competing with their business in your endeavors, they will usually cut you a deal. This unit set me back $5. I was looking for a unit that did not read discs but still contained a working power supply.

Console Surgery

I've removed the CD-ROM assembly and metal shielding (Figure 4-32).

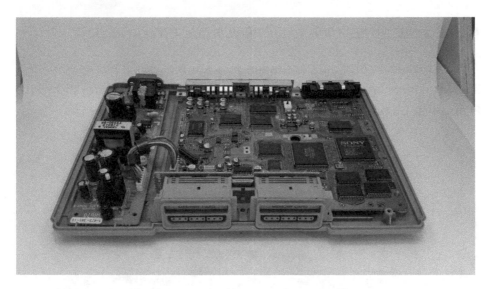

Figure 4-32. *Inside the SCPH-1001 model PlayStation 1*

I'll save the main CPU board and power supply. The main CPU board still works, so it will be saved, although it is not being utilized in the scope of this project. I used a rotary tool with a cutoff wheel to remove all the standoffs and screw mounts that support the main CPU board. Leave the power supply supports and mounts intact. This gives me a flat service to plan my layout and mount the Pi shown in Figure 4-33.

Figure 4-33. *All PlayStation SCPH-1001 guts removed except the power supply board*

Again, Thingiverse is a great resource. I found this USB mounting bracket (Figure 4-34) from user Retro_Emulation that fits in place of the PS1's memory card and controller ports.

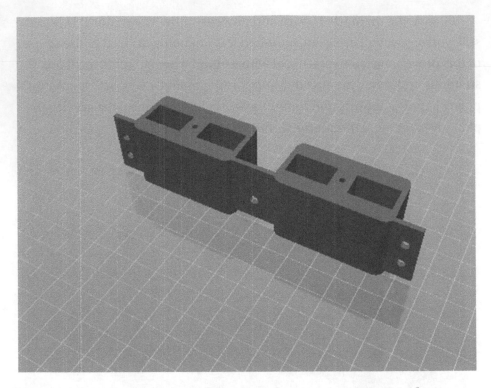

Figure 4-34. *Custom controller insert from user Retro_Emulation on thingiverse.com*

Buying these USB 3.0 extension cables is likely the most costly part in this mod, but the idea is the same; we need a front panel mount connection for USB controllers. I've painted this bracket gray as shown in Figure 4-35. Color matching the PS1 console gray was not in my plans; spray paint gray is close enough.

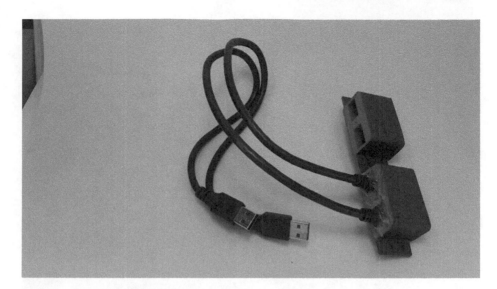

Figure 4-35. *3D Printed part with USB extensions hot glued in*

The front view of this 3D printer panel is shown in Figure 4-36. Again, not necessary; however this extra step does sell the look of a finished product. You could always model your own bracket to fit a controller port of your choosing. Using the model found on Thingiverse will get you all the dimensions you need to get started.

Figure 4-36. *Front view of replacement controller port for PS1*

The SCPH-1001 case is perfect for this application with its large cutout for RCA connections. Next we will mount the Pi so the HDMI, AV out, and USB power connections are accessible via the rear opening of the SCPH-1001 case. Using a drill (good) or a drill press (best), drill some M3 holes that match the Pi's four mounting holes. I've adjusted the locations a bit hence the extra holes (oops) shown in Figure 4-37. Insert four 17mm M3 female/female standoffs in the four holes.

Figure 4-37. *Standoffs to mount Raspberry in PS1 shell*

If you have 5V power supply suited for the Raspberry Pi, you could mount the Pi upside down, place the top cover back on, and mark this mod complete (preemptive Figure 4-38). However, I would like to take it a few steps further for authenticity's sake.

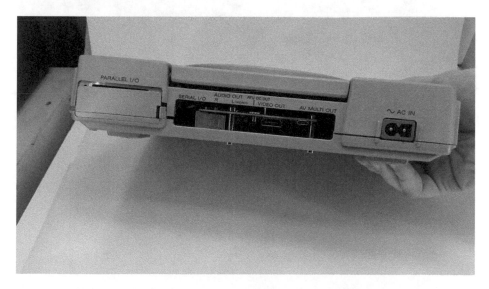

Figure 4-38. *Raspberry Pi access thanks to SCPH-1001 model rear cutout*

My goal is to utilize the PS1's power button, reset button, and the original power supply. The PS1 outputs 7.3V and 3.5V. Using a multimeter, we can verify the location of 7.3V and a ground connection like in Figure 4-39. Place the PS1's power supply back into the case and fasten it down with original screws that held it in place. Connect the power cord and use a multimeter (Figure 4-39) to identify the 7.6V pin and ground. Be mindful of where your hands are when handling this power supply PCB. Mains voltage is present in the areas shown in Figure 4-40. Do not touch this area when the power supply is plugged into main power.

Figure 4-39. *Locating usable voltage on PS1 power supply*

Figure 4-40. *Mains voltage (120VAC) on power supply*

Note   Figure 4-39 demonstrates a setup with exposed 120VAC. The underside of the PS1 power supply has live 120VAC. Use caution when probing the PCB and measuring DC voltages. Do not place this PCB on a conductive surface, like a metal table.

The RPi can only handle 5 volts at the USB input (more like 5.25V since it uses a cell phone charger power supply), so we need to step down the PS1's 7V to 5V using a buck converter or switching regulator. These modules are easily found on eBay or amazon.com for $1–$2 each. I've actually made a breakout PCB for this module (Figure 4-41), but more on the breakout PCB later. I'll mount this PCB in the case and power the Pi directly from its 5V and GND GPIO pins. To connect from the now regulated 5V and the RPi, some 22 AWG wire soldered to an extra-long female header is used to make a removable plug (Figure 4-42).

Figure 4-41. *eBay special step-down converter on a custom board*

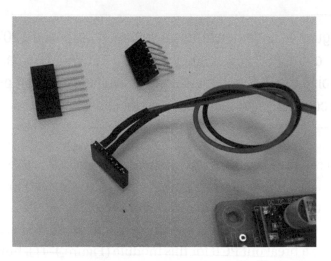

Figure 4-42. *Common female, extra-long header used as a plug*

I've added some heat shrink to insulate the wire and connector (Figure 4-43).

Note   I have skipped the first pin in the six-position header. Continue to follow along as this will be explained upon further.

Figure 4-43. *Add heat shrink to wires*

Mount voltage regulator with some M3 machine screws as seen in Figure 4-44.

Figure 4-44. *DC-DC step-down board placement in PS1*

Now, I should mention it's not really ideal to mix such a modern single-board computer with a power supply 20 years its senior. Do proceed with caution if trying the aforementioned method. The ~7VDC pin is meant to power the CD-ROM motor in charge of spinning the optical disc; the life expectancy of your PS1's power supply will vary. The early model PlayStations like the SCPH-100x series output 17watts. Later models like SCPH-5xxx and beyond consumed only 10watts. If a Raspberry Pi consumes 5V at 2A, that's already met our ceiling of power consumption. I do not recommend doing this with a newer model PlayStation. Practically speaking, it's not like Sony changed the PS1 supply to match the better efficiency; with that said, I have not tested a supply outside this SCPH-1001 model.

As an alternative, you could cut PCB traces and isolate the power switch on the PS1 power supply. After all we are in pursuit of reusing the PS1's power and reset button. Adding input jack on the rear of the case and a 5VDC wall adapter would accomplish the same feat with some cut traces and bypass wires soldered to the PS1's "Power" button connection.

Add the USB controller front-mount assembly and zip-tie this down using the horizontal vents on the right side (Figure 4-45).

Figure 4-45. *Mounting custom controller port into case*

Before we connect power to the PI, it's best to take some extra precaution. A mistake here will render your RPi useless. Using only the official raspberrypi.org GPIO pin out as a reference, I made a cheat sheet that identifies all the GPIOs and the power pins. I scaled this to size and printed it out like Figure 4-46.

Figure 4-46. *Raspberry Pi GPIO cheat sheet*

Since this cheat sheet matches the GPIO headers in size, I can push this paper print out into the headers and use it as a reference label. This way I never mix up 5V and ground (a $35+ mistake). These power and ground headers route past any reverse polarity protection and regulation. They are a direct link to the Broadcom CPU/GPU. Anything wired incorrectly here will destroy the Pi. Figure 4-47 is your *measure twice* insurance policy.

Figure 4-47. *Cheat sheet mounted to headers*

Connect the power leads to the Pi like in Figure 4-48. Verify you power the ground match your GPIO label cheat sheet. Is your cheat sheet correct? The top two pins on the right are 5V, and the third is ground. I skipped the first pin at the top right. That makes the second and third pin locations on our custom plug 5V and ground, respectively. It's common practice to wire a plug that connects with an edge reference, hence why we skipped the first GPIO pin. Shifting the plug down one pin is not good practice when establishing references.

Figure 4-48. *Power plug connected to GPIO headers*

The RPi will be mounted using M3 standoffs. Again, the location is not critical, only so the Pi's AV power can be accessed from the rear (Figure 4-49).

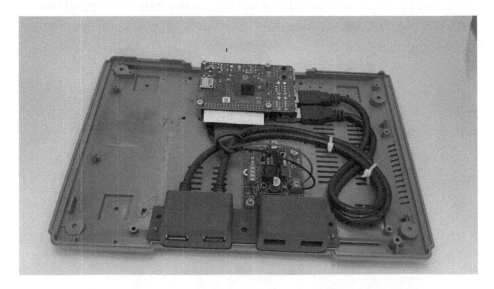

Figure 4-49. *Raspberry Pi mounted upside down on standoffs*

Remount the original power supply back in the bottom half and secure with the original screws like in Figure 4-50.

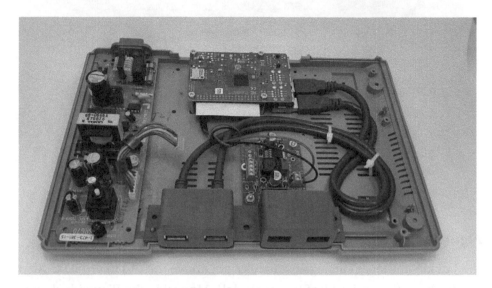

Figure 4-50. *Add power supply into case*

To keep everything modular, I inserted solid core wires into the original PS1 power supply Molex cable shown in Figure 4-51. As an alternative, you can solder this to the bottom of the PCB where the cable terminates if you wish.

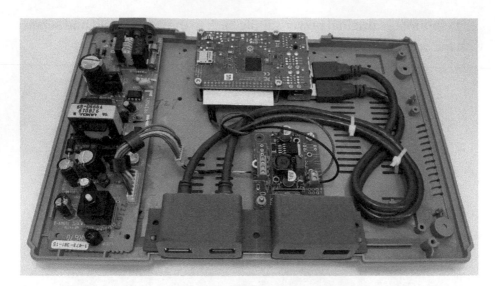

Figure 4-51.   *Power supply connection to step-down converter*

Luckily the laser carriage occupies right above the Pi's microSD card slot (only on this series PlayStation Model). Mounting the Pi upside down like this will give us somewhat easy access to the SD card (Figure 4-52). Sometimes we get lucky.

Figure 4-52.   *SD card access with lid open*

Fasten the top half of the PlayStation case with the original screws and enjoy your PlayStation-styled emulation console (Figure 4-53).

Figure 4-53. *Finished! Raspberry Pi in a PS1 shell*

Final Thoughts

Who knew something as simple as dressing up your naked Raspberry Pi had so many options? Remember, whatever enclosure route you decide to take, proceed with skepticism. According to the Raspberry Pi Foundation, since 2017 over 12.5 million units have been sold; and each one is a naked PCB. This creates a huge market for cases, many of which are just after your money. Read reviews and forums regarding which case is best and which to avoid. If you want to continue the DIY spirit, 3D print one or better yet make your own. Making your own custom case can be avenue of expression or just pure utility. Broken or unrepairable game consoles are a great starting project to repurpose some iconic plastic into a homage of retro gaming.

Summary

We've successfully brought back some life from a discarded (and broken) PlayStation 1 console by converting it into a custom case for our Raspberry Pi. This process was relatively easy because of some large open access panels already present on the case. The large roomy interior helped with cable management too. The majority of the work was relocating the Pi's side USB ports to the front of the console shell to match its aesthetics.

The same method can be applied to other consoles like the NES, Dreamcast, and so on. Just remember to abide by the unwritten rules of retro gaming. Never destroy a working console. Unrepairable consoles are around if you search for them. You won't score any good karma by reducing the limited supply of these cherished consoles by sacrificing an innocent console for your custom needs.

CHAPTER 5

Modern Fabrication Tools

Before we take a journey of building an arcade, it's time we familiarize ourselves with new tools. We are still making a wood arcade cabinet shell; however, the methods to achieve this will be new. Traditional tools are still applicable here and can be substituted to replicate these instructions; however, I do not expect one to match some of these modern techniques and capabilities of industrial tools. Traditional tools like a table saw, circular saw, jigsaw, and scroll saw are all substitutes, but there is one tool that will take your ambitions and open a new skill ceiling; that is computer-aided drafting (CAD), and we'll start with that. This is not a build-as-you-go guide; this is a structured and engineered arcade cabinet build.

CAD Overview

Most arcade build guides are kind enough to offer a template that you can redraw and transfer to your wood stock or print out and paste over your wood to then cut out. We can accomplish a template, but our goal with CAD is to design with production or economies of scale. In 2011, the idea of making a mini arcade kit was unheard of, and I wanted to share my passion. In order to accomplish this, new techniques and skills are required. The one-off hand tool process cannot match modern production tools and methods. Therefore, to complement an arcade model drafted in

© Mark Frauenfelder and Ryan Bates 2019
M. Frauenfelder and R. Bates, *Raspberry Pi Retro Gaming*,
https://doi.org/10.1007/978-1-4842-5153-9_5

CAD, we need an equally modern tool to produce the wood cabinet panels, a CNC machine. A CNC machine is a computer numerical controlled cutting tool. The process is as follows: start with a CAD drawing comprised of vector lines; using a post processor (sometimes integrated with the CNC machine software), you'll turn these vector lines into numerical coordinates. The CNC machine interprets these numerical coordinates and moves either a cutting tool through your material or, in this application, guides a focused CO_2-excited laser to perform the cutting. Designing with CAD and using an efficient tool like a laser cutter (Figure 5-1), we can produce intricate mini arcade cabinets with precision cut parts at high volumes. Tools like a laser cutter give you a glimpsed into industrial production.

Figure 5-1. *75-watt laser cutter with a 28x18-inch cutting bed*

I want to produce more than one of these arcades, so we are skipping over the one-off cabinet guides with rough cut wood and hand tools. We are going to draft a model based on parts that fit our scale, verify our model fits with the parts we've selected, transfer that 3D model into a vector template, and use a laser cutter to fabricate all the panels of our miniature arcade.

Q. "What CAD should I use to draw my arcade design?"

A. Whatever is available to you.

Because of the abundance of 3D CAD programs available, I'm only going to mention a few brief programs to get you started. The key takeaway is CAD takes time to learn, simply pick something and get started. If you're looking for something free and something you can grow your skills into, I would try Autodesk's AutoCAD Fusion 360. This is a free program that will get you started with some caveats in mind. It's a free license; therefore, you agree to the terms of use to not make money off of it. Some advanced features are locked away, but it is the best introduction to CAD. Because of the free-license model, you'll find plenty of support in the maker and DIY community. Fusion 360 is the best place to start 3D designing on a limited or nonexistent, hobbyist budget.

Tools like SolidWorks are incredibly robust in design, simulation, and analysis capabilities to do even more complex tasks. The trade-off is a very expensive license cost. Most universities with engineering programs teach SolidWorks. At their full commercial license, Fusion360 and SolidWorks are both extremely useful programs; the better choice is simply the one you become proficient in. Again, pick whatever is available to you and get started.

The amount of 2D CAD programs take a similar spread, two big commercial options but with more free and open source programs. If you're just looking for plane vector drawing I would encourage you to try the 100%-free, open source Inkscape program. Inkscape is mostly comparable to Corel Draw or Adobe Illustrator but with limitations of course. For reference, Abode Illustrator is the industrial standard of 2D vector and art programs, with Corel Draw taking up the rest of the market share. Licensing Adobe Illustrator or Corel Draw is not for the hobbyist. Inkscape offers the basic framework in regard to capabilities that Corel and Illustrator offer, but with less of a refined and familiar user interface. You can create 2D artwork and vector files (but nothing 3D) in Inkscape. Inkscape is where I started designing my arcades.

There's so much more to say about CAD programs, but in the effort to be concise and to focus on our build, I recommend you just start drawing in *any* CAD. The tools I started with were Inkscape, where I exclusively drew in 2D and had to mentally project my drawings into 3D. This was a steep learning curve and, as a result, produced lots of scraps and defunct designs as I went through the revision process. I recommend, if you want to get into laser cutting, always verify your models with a 3D model either in Fusion 360 or the like. You can find a legacy version of an old program called 123D by Autodesk. This is a stripped-down version of Fusion (before Fusion 360 was incentivized and Autodesk made a true free version of their 3D AutoCAD software), but it will still produce the same muscle memory and cognitive thinking 3D CAD requires. Autodesk's 123D is more of an introductory 3D CAD program, but still useful if you are just getting your bearings as an absolute beginner.

To wrap up this introduction of tools, I should emphasize by no means should you go out and purchase a laser cutter. This is an absolute sticker-shock tool and even I don't own one (apartment living also does not help my case). If you're fortunate enough to be in a large city, you might also discover a makerspace in your area. Local makerspaces may have a laser cutter, and this is probably the best place to pursue this tool. If you find yourself with a large warehouse or basement and you have a spare $10k to $40k, purchasing a laser cutter might be for you. Laser cutters cut with essentially concentrated heat and fire. These tools require exhaust ventilation—your basement workspace might need a bit of an update. If buying one is really your game, to cut 1/4 inch wood at a respectable speed, start pricing at 80 watts. The tube is significantly longer (around 49 inches) on an 80-watt machine compared to the entry-level 40-watt (27 inches) machines. This means the machine footprint is also inherently larger. A 40-watt machine is a desktop-sized cutter; at 80 watts you'll be at a free-standing machine size. In any regard, the capabilities of a laser cutter machine are astonishing once you get familiar. You'll wish you spec'd something you can grow into; 80 watts give you headroom to do so.

The bed size really just depends on the machine footprint and how much space you can allot for this machine. Granted the cost of one laser cutter could get you a fully furnished woodshop or a new car, you don't need to own one to experience it. (I actually don't own one.) You can always outsource laser cutting or (the best option) find a makerspace that has one. If you do some online searching, you can find some reputable outlets that can do laser cutting as a contract work. However, I encourage getting hands-on time with one of these machines; they are quite fascinating.

Finally, I want to introduce one tool that is critical for building on the small of scale. With resources like CAD that let you draw and dimension parts to create a model, we need a tool that can measure with precision. Calipers. You don't need a fancy set. In Figure 5-2, the top shows a cheap Harbor Freight 6 inch digital caliper.

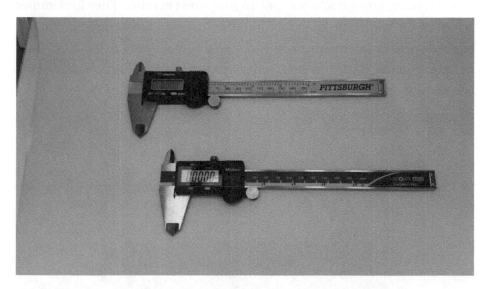

Figure 5-2. *Calipers*

These usually are around the $15 range and will perform adequately for our application. Illustrating what's available on the other end of the spectrum, pictured bottom in Figure 5-2 is a Mitutoyo digimatic caliper;

these are around the $120–$160 range. Our design tolerance doesn't get close to the thousandth inch range (0.001″), but if you go beyond the hundredth inch (0.01″) precision level in your future, I would look outside the Harbor Freight tool realm.

Wood Selection

Quarter inch or 0.25″ nominal plywood is the best material for this type of build. You'll likely encounter 5mm- or 6mm-thick wood at your local brick and mortar hardware store. Regarding wood, the you-get-what-you-pay-for mantra applies here; however, we can cut corners and hide a substandard grade of plywood with good paint job. If it matters to you, buy the quality 1/4″ plywood like Maple or Birch plywood. Maple and birch plywood hover around $26–$32 per 4ft x 8ft sheet at retail. They look rather nice from the hardware store as is, but of course you are paying for that finished surface. Once your paint and finishing skills are up to par, try the cheaper Chinese-sourced wood underlayment. Figure 5-3 shows a side by side of what these look like on the surface.

Figure 5-3. *Birch and underlayment plywood*

The Birch (left) has a smooth, uniformly sanded finish of, well, Birch plywood. The underpayment plywood (right) has a somewhat smooth and somewhat uniform surface.

Flipping these samples over (ignore the burn marks from the laser cutter), Figure 5-4 presents a clearer detail of what we are paying for. The Birch sample (left) maintains a finished veneer surface.

Figure 5-4. *Underside of birch and underlayment plywood*

In contrast, the underlayment shows the veneer inconsistencies of some sort of hardwood; these are the knots and likely to be in abundance in lower-grade plywood especially for subfloor plywood. Because of their hardness, these knots tend to fall out during the shaving process that creates the veneer layer. This knot (and every knot) is slightly recessed and presents as an imperfection that would have to be filled prior to painting either with a wood-type or paintable filler.

Let's look at a cross section of these samples shown in Figure 5-5. Birch plywood is on the top and the underlayment is at the bottom. The Birch veneer is much thicker than the underlayment veneer. The inner ply is also much denser and uniform and is likely genuine wood (note the wavy, ring layer passing through). The underlayment (bottom) has a barely visible veneer which is prone to chipping. Sand this too much and you'll break into the middle plywood layer. The middle ply is usually a wood/paper/filler mix. This nonuniform layer is not bonded together nearly as well as the higher-grade plywood and can sometimes cause issues on small intricate laser-cut parts. There are also more void present in the underlayment, which is again acceptable for the grade of plywood (subflooring). These live edges can be unreliable when painting and finishing unless you have a good body/wood filler that primes and bonds the surface.

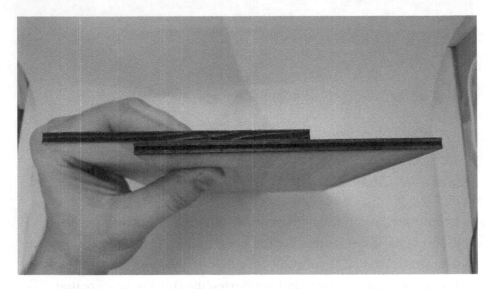

Figure 5-5. *Cross section of birch and underlayment plywood*

Lastly, and this is a more precautionary tale, underlayment plywood (depending on where it's sourced) will likely contain a formaldehyde-based glue. Saw blade cutting is okay, but laser cutting (burning) could result in toxic vapors. Always use proper ventilation when laser cutting.

Component Selection

The key to designing any arcade is to frame the most critical component. The monitor. I mean this in the most literal sense: We need to identify and source a monitor that will fit our scale, measure its specific dimensions and frame an arcade around it. I am focusing on specifically arcade's bezel thickness and keeping to an appropriate to the scale the arcade with the monitor. In layman's terms, no matter the size of the screen, a thick bezel bordering the screen makes the arcade monitor look small and consequently the rest of the arcade fit in the acidic size that the monitor frames the cabinet within.

Note   I am building this mini arcade on a 1:8 scale. The tips and tricks explained from here on can be applied to an arcade build large or small. The key here is proportions.

The scale I'm working at is around 1:8. This is based on one critical factor—how wide the control panel is for one player. This design constraint coincides with the maximum LCD size we can fit comfortably in this scale which is about 10 inch diagonal. It's possible to fit a larger monitor, but this 10.1 inch LCD seems to be the most prevalent size in the DIY community as manufactures continue to produce this OEM part in high volume. In Figure 5-6 is a 10.1 inch diagonal LCD screen with a resolution of 1024 x 800, and you can still find it on eBay or Amazon for under $70.

Figure 5-6. *Original equipment from manufacturer (OEM) 10.1 inch LCD*

Another convenient factor is the HDMI input shown in the driver PCB in Figure 5-7. Already we have a perfect candidate to use with the Raspberry Pi.

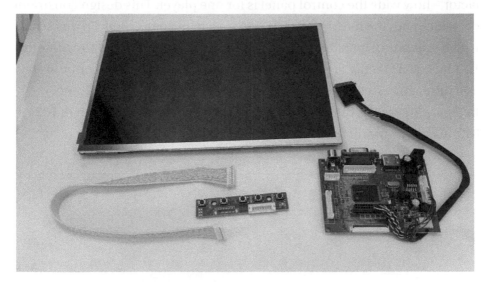

Figure 5-7. *LCD with driver PCB*

144

Design Pre-planning

I will start drawing this arcade in 2D. Once we have some cornerstone features set, you can transition to 3D to verify all parts mesh and fit with each other. I will follow the same practice: draw key arcade panels in 2D, move these key parts into a 3D model and finish the design in 3D. A good design process breaks up the overall goal (design/build an arcade) into smaller, manageable chunks. Before we start assembling an arcade, we need to focus on a few details like:

- Monitor/LCD size?

- Control panel size (number of players?)

- Speaker size: Fills a room with music or just enough volume for the person playing it?

- Profile design or theme?

- Joystick and arcade button hardware: US or Japanese?

Answering the aforementioned questions will narrow down the overall size of the arcade and give us some guidelines to consider when formulating a design. Breaking these points down further will give us more manageable goals. With a stronger focus on detail, we can get a better understanding of our design and what direction to pursue solutions within it. A strong focus on detail looks like:

- Monitor/LCD size?

  - How to mount the LCD?

- Control panel size (number of players?)

  - How many buttons per player: Two buttons for games from the 1980s or six buttons for fighting games like Capcom fighting games?

- Speaker size: Fills a room with music or just enough volume for the person playing it?
    - Speaker location: Under Marquee or buried in cabinet?
- Profile design or theme?
    - Unique features: Storage space for battery pack?
- Joystick and arcade button hardware: US or Japanese?

Let's solve the LCD task. For a mini arcade, a LCD with a diagonal measurement of 10 inches will make a cabinet about 1/8 scale.

I like to start my designs by framing the LCD and its surrounding bezel. You'll want to measure the overall size of your LCD (case) and then the viewable area (window) and translate this into a drawing like in Figure 5-8. Be sure to create a bezel large enough to mount the LCD to the back of the rear of this panel, but not too much that it crowds the focus of the viewable area. Don't put too much stock in this yet, we are just framing the LCD with bezel. Find a ratio that "looks good." A giant bezel that crowds the screen misdirects the players' attention from the business end of the cabinet, the screen. An unnecessarily thin bezel can present design woes later, like a cramped control panel or not enough cabinet structure to mount the LCD and contain the rest of the arcades' parts.

I've drawn a bezel that has a surface area of under 2:1 to the viewable area of the screen. It might seem a lot, but at this scale, it's just right. The viewable area of the LCD is 8.6"x 5.4" = 46.4in^2 and the bezel comes out to 10.5"x 8.3" = 87.2 in^2. This ratio is closer to 8:15, but that number is not very helpful. Again, if it looks good and there is enough border to bolt to and build a cabinet around, go with that.

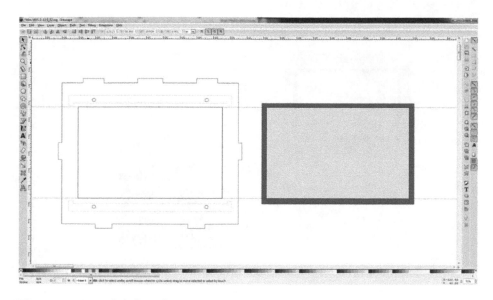

Figure 5-8. *LCD bezel sizing*

Now that I have the driving width of the cabinet defined, set by the LCD bezel, I want to draw the next anchor point that determines the overall feature set of the cabinet. This is the final anchor that nails our proportions at this scale, and that is the control panel or where all the action happens from the player's input (button presses and joystick movements). With the LCD drawn to scale and framed, next I am going to dimension the control panel to match this width plus this thickness of the cabinet side panels (add 2 x 0.25 inches) with some overhang. Hopefully this measurement signifies the control panel will be at least comfortable. If not, time to revise either the LCD bezel size or go with a larger monitor. Our LCD selection has given us a width around 11 inches, or about the width of the mini keyboard (a keyboard sans the number pad). This is acceptable, but again can be subjective depending on your level of comfort and play style.

I recommend the standard six-button layout with a slight curvature that matches the tips of your index, middle, and ring fingers. Layouts like Figure 5-9 are rather subjective, so design a layout that is conformable for you and matches your end use.

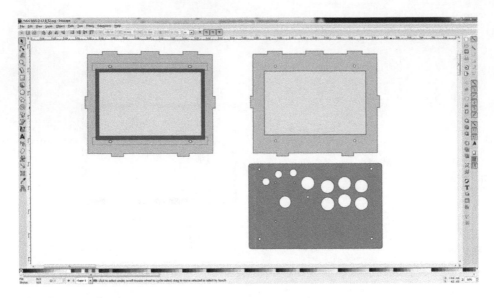

Figure 5-9. *Bezel and control panel sizing*

Only playing 1980s console games? You won't need more than four dedicated buttons (A,B, Start, Select). Focusing on arcade fighting games? Plan for six dedicated buttons plus two extras for 'Coin' and '1-Player Start'.

Arcade Hardware

Before you model that control panel, let's talk about what hardware to populate it. Arcade buttons and joysticks are really about preference, feel, and play style. If you're not sure, read on to learn the major differences between the US and Japanese part manufactures. Once you're familiar, take a trip to an arcade and decide what you like best. you've probably never paid second mind to it, but the feel of the control plays a big part in the experience.

I've modeled this arcade with 30mm diameter Sanwa buttons (pictured on the right in Figure 5-10); the other style from across the globe are Suzo-Happ (pictured left) buttons with a threaded nylon nut.

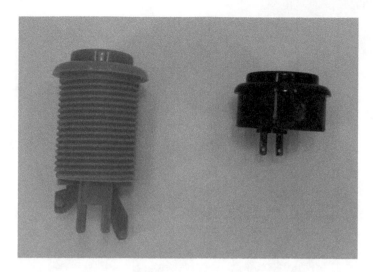

Figure 5-10. *Suzo-Happ (left), Sanwa arcade button*

These Suzo-Happ buttons are great for sandwiching layers like a clear acrylic layer + artwork layer + wood backing layer together. They are most common in arcade cabinet with American origins. The Suzo-Happ buttons offer a robust solution to games that will see heavy and hard use over time. The long body fits into thick control panels, and the nylon nuts keep it from being removed easily. The microswitches can be replaced independent of the button; they're great for servicing in heavily used arcades. Another feature is the convex top—again more preference, but still a feature. See Figure 5-11 nylon and microswitch assembly of Suzo-Happ vs. Sanwa arcade button.

Figure 5-11. *Suzo-Happ (left), Sanwa arcade button with microswitch*

Standard Sanwa buttons have a slightly softer and shorter throw when pressed and therefore a faster actuation microswitch. In contrast, you'll likely always find Sanwa or Seimitsu joystick and button hardware in Japanese "candy" cabinets, like the Aero City or Astro City units by Sega.

Joysticks are another beast, and inherently more complex.

The two main joystick flavors are ball-top joysticks and bat-top joysticks respectively originating in Japan and US manufacturing. Ball-top joysticks are almost universally found in Japanese arcade cabinets or candy cabinet. Figure 5-12 shows bat-top on the left and ball-top joysticks on the right.

Figure 5-12. *Suzo-Happ (left) and Sanwa joystick (right)*

Ball-top joysticks are usually shorter in length and have a lighter microswitch pressure and inherently a shorter throw range to activate the microswitches. All-time joysticks are usually light-resistance and agile-input devices. Common ball-top joystick brands are Sanwa and Seimitsu. Pictured right is a Sanwa JFL-TP-8Y joystick. Ball-top joysticks have the ability to limit directional inputs by adding different gates on the bottom (Figure 5-13).

Figure 5-13. *Underside of Suzo-Happ (left) and Sanwa joystick (right)*

The gate on the bottom of the joystick allows you to lock out directions. For example, if you were playing PacMan, you'd only want four directions to register: up, down, left, and right. A "gate" can restrict the actuators movement to block out the other diagonals. You would not want to accidentally trigger a diagonal while playing PacMan—hence the use for gates.

Bat-top joysticks are extremely common in most American arcade cabinets and a common choice for both American and Japanese fighting arcade games like Mortal Kombat, Street Fighter, and Tekken. Bat-top joysticks are usually taller and the stick is shaped more like a baseball bat with a taper that widens toward the top. The return-to-neutral spring is usually stiffer; therefore, the throw takes more force to activate the microswitches in this joystick. The major brand for these joysticks is Suzo-Happ, and their standard is the Competition Joystick which is pretty standard an arcade cabinet hardware. These joysticks are very robust and rugged and can take extreme punishment which is usually why they are always installed exclusively in fighting games. The biggest complaint of bat top is a result of the stiffer throw. It's harder to perform fast-input-window rotational commands like special moves in fighting games.

There's so much more to joysticks, but really the rest is about preference and highly subjective. To continue, we need to select a joystick type, ball-top in this case because the footprint is smaller (and happens to be my preferred feel). Now we can layout the control panel. In summary, I've selected six dedicated Sanwa buttons and a Sanwa JFL ball-top joystick.

Once you decide on a layout, I recommend printing out the control panel at 1:1 scale and getting your hands on it, literally. This is our practical form of measurement. Is what shown in Figure 5-14 comfortable? I've got a pre-cut version already, and this is about as small as I'll go in respect to my comfort and play style.

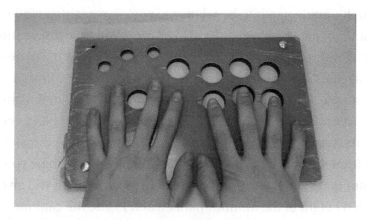

Figure 5-14.   *Control panel "size and feel" test*

If it feels too small, this is the best time to make adjustments in the width of your arcade or just widen the control panel. If it's not comfortable, why bother playing it?

With these two key components framing the arcade cabinets design, I then move on to the profile of the arcade which stylize the entire cabinet from now on. Shown in Figure 5-15 are a few different profiles that I've designed over the years which give different characteristics and themes for arcade cabinets.

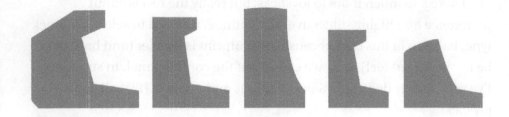

Figure 5-15. *Mini arcade profile ideas*

The last cornerstone of our cabinet design is the monitor viewing angle. Arcades rarely mount the monitor perpendicular to the floor like a PC monitor. You're more likely to look down slightly from where your head is so this angle needs to be relative to your eye position while looking down at a slight angle. Your head will likely be positioned above this arcade LCD with your nose pointed down slightly to view it. We need to tilt the LCD bezel back slightly to match this. I've chosen about 14 degrees for this example. In order to determine this now angled panel within the cabinet's overall size, we need to look at it from a different perspective. Take the front view of the monitor bezel you've drawn, and translate it as if viewed from the side like Figure 5-16. Rotate this to the angle you want the monitor to rest, in this case 14 degrees. This translation will give you the adjusted height of the monitor panel when inside the cabinet. Adding reference lines will allow you to locate where interlocking cross braces should be placed.

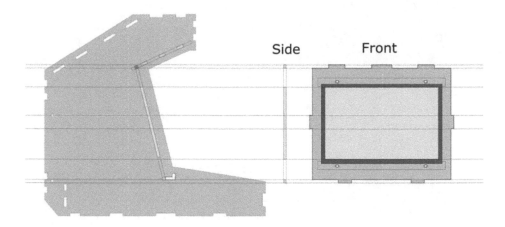

Figure 5-16. *Translating an angle piece to mate with another panel*

The rest of the features can be designed a la carte as you get closer to the finished product. The monitor bezel is the driving dimensions that the arcade should be drawn to. The rest of the cabinet's features should be in proportion to this panel. I have two characteristics in mind that I want to focus on: first are speakers overhanging the control panel akin to traditional full-size arcades (a difficult feature at this scale) and significant storage space for additional electronics like a battery pack. I've chosen this profile in Figure 5-17 because it closely imitates a very iconic arcade cabinet.

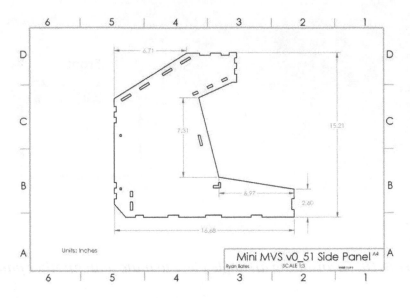

Figure 5-17. *Ryan's mini MVS design*

This cabinet style is going to closely match the North American four-slot arcade, which was an iconic machine for the American arcade industry. Now I understand everyone's nostalgia aligns with different arcade hardware styles, but at this point if you're open to CAD software, you should be able to draft up a design that suits your needs and wants.

The rest of this arcade design involves dozens of hours in CAD drawing around components that interlock with each other. Other features like removable access doors, mechanically fixed control panels, and shelves for extra internal storage will be explained later with the aid of a 3D model. Because our main tool focus is a laser cutter, I'm going to avoid any straight butt joints and make these all finger joint (interlocking panels) like in Figure 5-18.

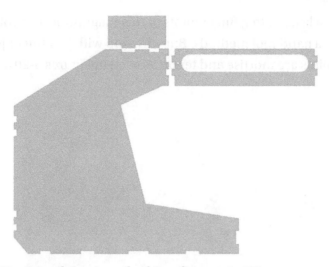

Figure 5-18. *Matching interlocking fingers in 2D*

Finger joints will not only allow for a larger surface area for glue to adhere to connecting parts but will also allow self-aligning and squaring of many of our panels when we come to clamp it all together. These finger joint alignments are verified in Figure 5-19.

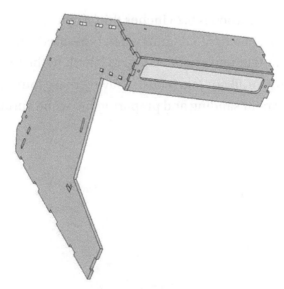

Figure 5-19. *Verifying Interlocking fingers in 3D*

Without a laser cutter, finger joints of this magnitude and volume are unfeasible via hand tool methods. But why stop with just finger joints? The rest of our joints are mortise and tenon as seen in Figures 5-20 and 5-21.

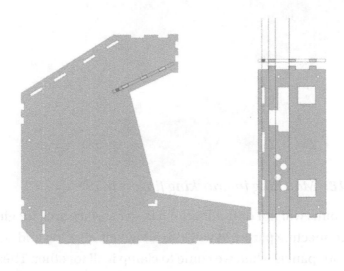

Figure 5-20. *Aligning and layout of LCD cross bracket in 2D*

Remember, if our wood is 0.25 inches thick (that 1/4 inch *nominal* wood is actually 0.21 inches (5.33mm) when measured with our calipers), our finger joints and tenons should equal in length to the thickness of our wood. This will make all our joints flush. Having these joints mate flush will reduce time spent sanding and preparing the wood surface for paint.

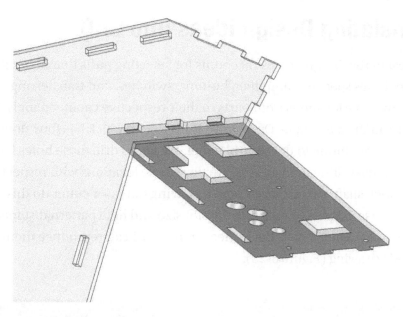

Figure 5-21. *Layout of LCD cross brackets 3D*

You could hand cut the finger and mortise and tenon joints ala Roy Underhill style; however, we've designed this cabinet to tolerances of hundreds of an inch, and it's incredibly laborious to produce this precision without a CNC machine.

So again, I emphasize a laser cutter because this build will only be as good as our least accurate tool. From now on, we are measuring components using calipers and transferring these dimensions into CAD drawings. You'll want to maintain a standard level of precision when we come to the physical product, hence a CNC machine or laser cutter in this example.

Translating Design Ideas into CAD

The rest of the design process accounts for selecting parts that fit our scale. This includes speakers, amplifier, buttons, switches, and transferring mounting hole locations from parts to their respective cabinet panels. Let's walk through an example. Our Sanwa JFL-TP-8Y joystick has four slots meant for mounting to the control panel. We could drill these holes later, but if we invest little time to measure these hole locations with respect to the joystick shaft, we can save a step by having our laser cutter do this.

I will use calipers to measure the slot size and hole pattern distance (Figure 5-22). Once I have these measurements, I can reproduce them in our CAD drawing (Figure 5-23).

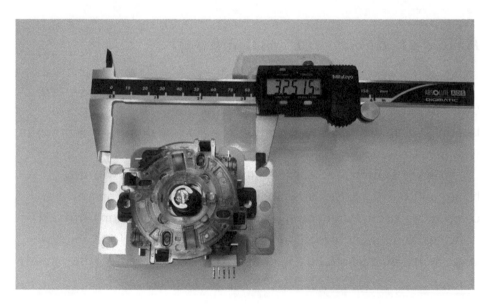

Figure 5-22. *Measuring hole layout spacing with calipers*

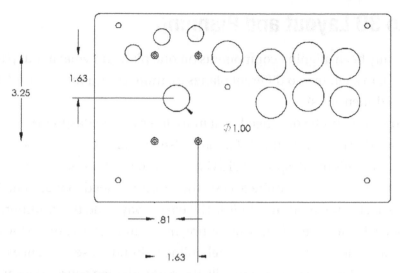

Figure 5-23. *Joystick mounting layout*

Repeating these steps for the audio amplifier, LCD driver PCB, and so on will make assembly even faster. The goal here is if you can eliminate using a tool you're already stuck using, do that. This is not one of those "a flat blade screwdriver will work as a chisel" examples. This is investing in our CAD drawing and getting the returns on a more capable tool, the laser cutter. Mounting holes can be done with a drill, but done in our drawing will help us position the joystick based on its footprint and better plan out the control panel. We can adjust alignment with the arcade buttons, space things out more, or condense the layout to fit more buttons if we know the size of things and create an accurate drawing. The time spent laser cutting these holes will always be faster than drilling them.

I will continue this process with items like our speakers and amplifier. you'll have to measure with your calipers and transfer these measurements into your drawing. Of course, this task isn't absolutely necessary. If you know the components will fit, you can always use a hand drill to make these holes later. But if you can do it in CAD level, invest in the CAD model because the laser cutter will reap your investment. I am going to production-level quantities with an end-user assembly experience like Ikea furniture. No drilling, all holes are present.

2D to 3D Layout and Planning

We've only been aligning components on one plan, but what about parts that have to align in two different planes or, more commonly referred, align in three dimensions?

More complex layouts need a bit more finesse. The Raspberry Pi's mounting holes are straightforward. Use the same technique as the previous. It's the Raspberry Pi's USB and Ethernet ports that need attention. These ports require access; therefore, we need to make cutouts with respect to the mounting holes. The easier way to do this is import a Raspberry Pi model to identify mounting holes and access ports. However, if you can't find a decent CAD model online to build these references, then we can do it the hard way. Thankfully the perks of open source design save us a few steps. There is a fully dimensioned Raspberry Pi on Raspberry Pi Foundation's web site: `www.raspberrypi.org/documentation/hardware/raspberrypi/mechanical/README.md`

The important dimensions in Figure 5-24 are the mounting holes laid-out in a rectangular pattern and the clearance distance needed for the I/O ports on the right of this mounting pattern.

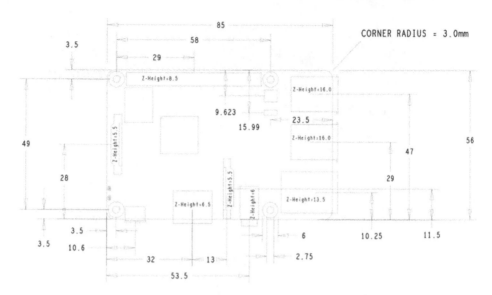

Figure 5-24. *Raspberry Pi mechanical drawing from raspberrypi.org*

I have translated the side view of the Raspberry Pi using the written dimensions of the I/O port heights from the mechanical drawing. The length the PCB is the same if we use our alignment as reference.

I've laid the respective panels aligned with the critical dimensions in Figure 5-25.

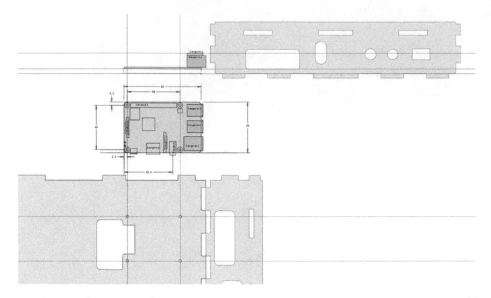

Figure 5-25. *Two perspective (2D) mounting the Pi*

Pictured on the lower half, I've aligned with respect to the mounting holes; the upper portion of the figure aligns to the side view with respect to the height of the PCB, USB, and Ethernet ports. I am using a riser plate (piece of wood) to life the RPIs I/O ports up about 0.21 inches. With these two views, we can draw a port cutout on the rear panel. Combining these two different perspectives produces our layout in 3D. If we move this to 3D, we can verify things with the help of an accurate RPi model and cabinet assembly (Figure 5-26). While we are here, I've also added a cutout on the bottom panel so there is easy access to the SD card.

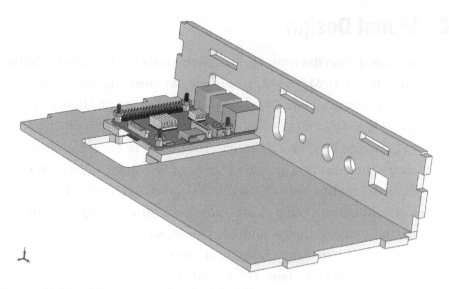

Figure 5-26. *RPi mount checked in 3D*

Fitting the rest of electronic components like the speakers and amplifier requires more of the same process. Measure hole locations with your calipers and transfer these measurements into your drawing. Draw the footprint of the part over the panel you plan to mount to verify if it fits and does not interfere with the rest of your assembly. All these hole layouts are not absolutely necessary. If you know the components will fit, you can always use a hand drill to make these holes later. But if you plan the layout within the CAD level, do so. Invest in the CAD model because the laser cutter will reap your investment. Checking how parts fit in 3D will save you from wasting material and time (or money) spent cutting. The design process is about the planning and checking. My intention is production-level quantities with an end-user assembly experience similar to Ikea furniture. No drilling, all holes are present.

LCD Mount Design

Based on experience, the most cumbersome process in arcade building is mounting the LCD. My best advice is use the most common, standard parts and package available. This means if you can get an OEM TFT panel, great! If you can't, say you have a PC monitor, strip it down until you get to the bare TFT assembly. The goal is to mount what was engineered to be mounted, meaning the bare TFT that comes off the factory line. Before this bare TFT is sold to brands like Dell, HP, Asus, and before said brands, put a plastic mold on it. Attempting to mount a monitor in its plastic shell is difficult. Our minds work best in plain three coordinates with right angles. That's not different in this design. Hopefully you've picked a bare TFT LCD display meant for laptop or tablet screen replacements. This unremarkable rectangular shell is easy to mount. Here's how I mount the LCD in Figure 5-27.

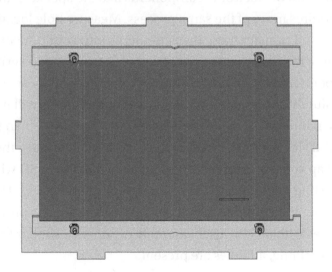

Figure 5-27. *LCD TFT mount layer 1*

Fortunately, its thickness is less than the stock thickness of our wood (0.21 inches), so we can use the sandwich method to mount it. Bubble wrap or foam tape can be applied to the TFT for the next layer shown in Figure 5-28. This will keep the TFT in place.

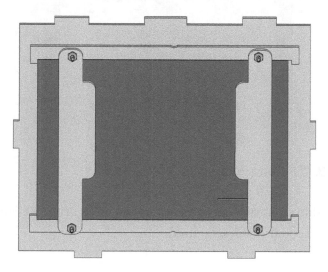

Figure 5-28. *TFT mount layer 2*

We need one more panel to attach the LCD driver PCB. It's tethered by a short cord, so best practice says to keep it close to the LCD. Another layer shown in Figure 5-29 works well. Note there is clearance for the screw heads between this panel and the LCD.

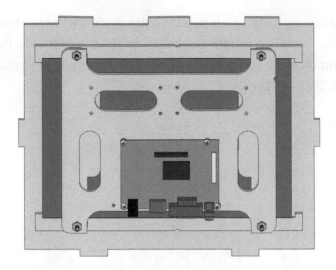

Figure 5-29. *TFT mount layer 3*

Here's a side cross section of all our layers in Figure 5-30. Four 1.25″ length screws keep this stack secured.

Figure 5-30. *Cross section of LCD mount, layers 1-3*

Despite all the business on the back, we have a clean from bezel with only four screw heads shown in Figure 5-31. This mounting method works very well if you want to add a clear acrylic bezel layer to sandwich some artwork OR a full acrylic sheet to protect the LCD (and add artwork also).

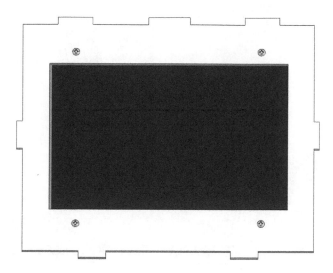

Figure 5-31. *Front view of LCD mounted in bezel panel*

Control Panel Features

I'll leave custom button layouts to the end user since that's a pretty subjective design choice. For now, we are sticking with six dedicated action buttons per player and a few extra buttons for start/select/coin-assigned inputs. Outside those basic requirements, I want to reserve this section to give us a couple quality-of-life improvements regarding the control panel. There are two goals here: The first being we want the control panel to always sit with tight and secure fit. With heavy playing there shouldn't be any small movement or knocking of the control panel where it sits with the cabinet frame. The control panel will remain a separate piece from the arcade to keep with traditions of easy access for maintenance. However, we still need a way to lock the panel down so it does not lift from the cabinet during play. Shown in Figure 5-32 is the method I've come up with that adds minimal laser cut parts and additional hardware.

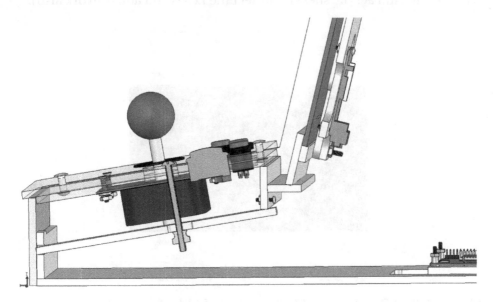

Figure 5-32. *Control panel with locking bracket installed*

This design also accommodates right-handed and left-handed mirror flips of the control panel, so if you want your joystick on the right, you can still use this locking bar mechanism (Figure 5-33).

Figure 5-33. *Through-view of control panel with locking bar*

The only additional hardware is a somewhat long screw (about 2.5 inches) and a knurled thumb screw to fasten everything down (both optional). Also helpful is a rubber band (drawn in Figure 5-34) to keep the locking bar in place when you add the long screw (Figure 5-35).

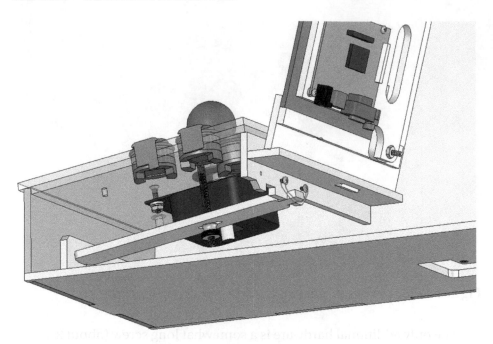

Figure 5-34.   Rubber band to retain locking bar

The plate that locks the part from the front of the arcade can be flipped to shift the lock bar for joystick mirror control panels. This means the joystick is on the right when playing; since my control panels are symmetrical along their vertical axis relative to how they nest in the cabinet, this design remains versatile.

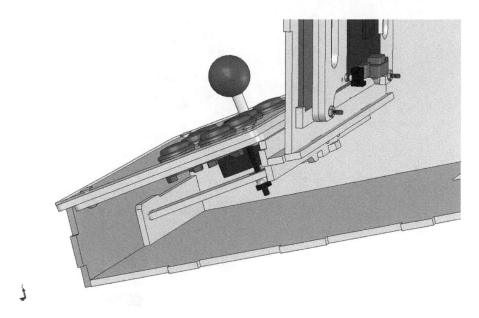

Figure 5-35. *Locking bar with screw*

While we are still on the subject on the control panel, let's add another feature: an acrylic top to protect from wear and tear, greasy hands, and great method to hold artwork. The easiest way here is to use binding posts. These are like male screws that mate with a female screw. See the cutaway view in Figure 5-36.

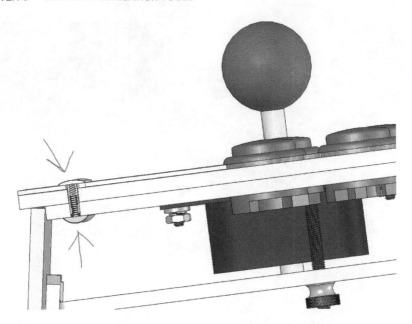

Figure 5-36. *Binding post-securing control panel layers*

Some last tricks remaining are how to fasten the joystick. I'm using flat head screws in Figure 5-37, so you'll still need a drill to countersink the joystick mounting holes.

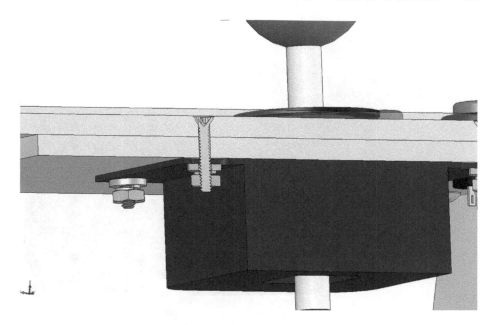

Figure 5-37. *Countersink with flat head screws*

To keep the joystick secure and the nuts from loosening during heated play, I'm going to add some lock washers or split washers in place. Tightening these split washers down (sandwich between the nut and washer) will add some extra friction force on the nut and prevent it from coming loose. See Figure 5-38 for this washer + split washer + nut assembly.

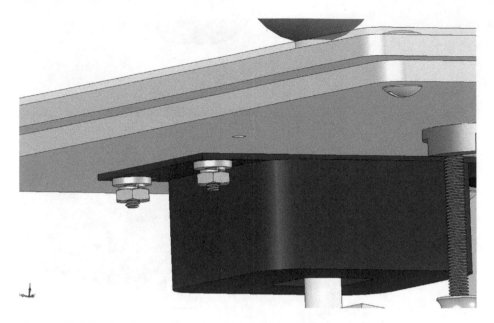

Figure 5-38. *Lock washers and nuts to screw joystick*

Design Review

Let's review our design checklist:

- Monitor/LCD size? **10.1″.**

  - How to mount the LCD? **Sandwich style.**

- Control panel size (number of players?) **11 inches, 1 player.**

  - How many buttons per player: two buttons for games from the 1980s or six buttons for fighting games like fighting games? **six dedicated buttons.**

- Speaker size: Fills a room with music or just enough volume for the person playing it? **Just enough for the person playing.**

176

- Speaker location: Under Marquee or buried in cabinet? **Both because I already did both and am writing in retroactively**.

- Profile design or theme? Four-slot arcade.

  - Unique features: Storage space for battery pack? **Sure. It's almost portable, so it should have a battery, I guess**.

- Joystick and arcade button hardware: US or **Japanese? Japanese joystick and buttons because we can't spare the room on such a small scale.**

OK, I think we are ready to build the rest of the cabinet. I mean it's basically just a box, so let's make a box. What you're looking at in Figure 5-39 is the result of lots of time. I've been building mini arcades for nearly 10 years. And here we are.

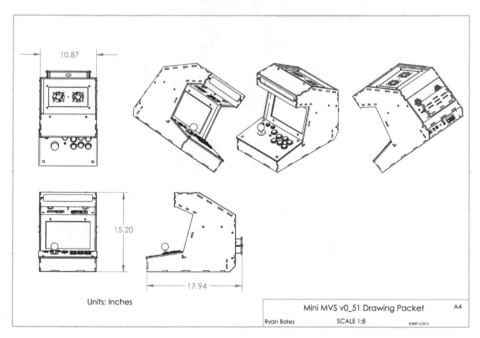

Figure 5-39. *Ryan's mini MVS drawing proof*

There are a lot of nuances that go into arcade cabinet designing on this scale. The design you're looking at rests on the shoulders of about five other previous cabinet models (Figure 5-40), all totaling hundreds of different revisions and dozens of different cabinets being constructed.

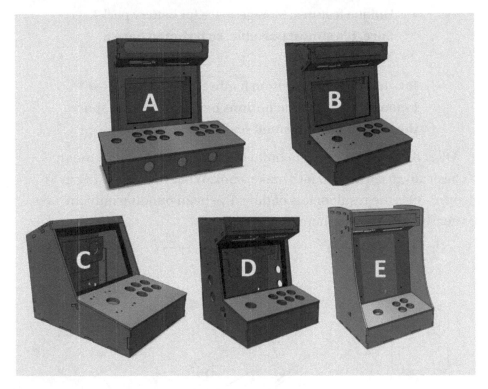

Figure 5-40. *Ryan's pervious mini arcade designs*

I usually don't know what works or looks good until I make it. Sometimes you just have to put in the time to get that polish. Here's the end result in Figure 5-41.

Figure 5-41. *Cut sheet for Ryan's mini MVS arcade*

This layout shows one particular example in regard to the tool that I'm using to cut these parts—laser cutter. I have nested all my parts so I can maximize the yield from my wood sheet. This cabinet fits on one sheet of 4x8ft plywood. I've also split my nest parts into five small sub-sections or sub-sheets. I've condensed these into five sub-sheets of a particular size. This is 24x16 inches which just so happens to be a common size that will fit in most of the laser cutters I have access to. This cabinet design with this many pieces (44+) on an 80-watt laser cutter takes about 45 minutes to cut start to finish. That estimate implies your drawing is fully prepped, the laser cutter is 100% functional and your wood stock is pre-cut and ready for production. If you ever send out your arcade cabinet drawing files to get laser cut by a light manufacture, they will likely quote on two factors: Set up time and machine time. Set up time is prepping the raw material stock. Machine time is how long the laser is running or time spent actually cutting through wood. If you're using someone else's laser, there are tips to save some cutting time and that's to share cut lines. If you have two identical lines that overlap, why cut them twice? Instead of having the overlapping line defined twice by two separate parts, delete one instance of the overlap so the laser cutter doesn't cut that line twice. Here's an example in Figure 5-42.

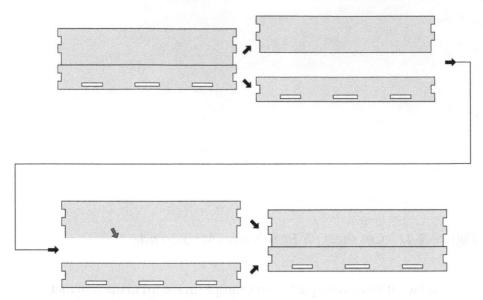

Figure 5-42. *Sharing cut lines and reducing cut redundancy*

Figure 5-42 shows where to delete a repeated line that is already cut. Note it shares a boundary with another part. In this application (80watt, laser cutting 1/4″ wood), that saves us about 9 seconds of machine time. Clean up your drawing and resolve all these instances; you might save a few minutes. I've been staring at this design long enough to say there's about 151 inches that can be saved on redundant cuts. To get that into perspective in overhead costs, let's use Pololu.com laser cutting service as a control. At the time of this writing, Pololu.com charges $0.15 per linear inch of cutting. So, one could save $22.65 on outsourcing with a bit of touch-up in their cut file. Suppose you're saying, "Ryan, why not reduce the complexity of the arcade cabinet and not cut so many parts to save money?" Great question. Speaking of complexity, let's actually build this thing!

Figure 5-43 shows we've got all our parts cut from our design.

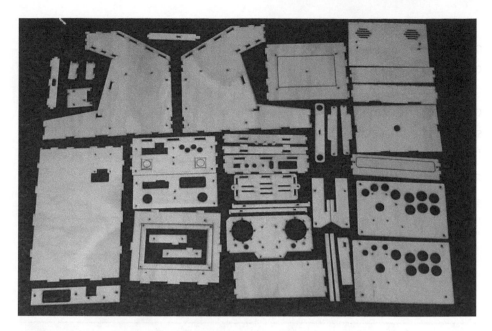

Figure 5-43. *Cut parts, ready for assembly*

Wood Cabinet Assembly

Before we can assemble, I want to go over some basic tools needed to assemble this cabinet:

- Wood glue (Tightbond, use nothing else)

- Damp rag for glue cleanup

- Phillips screwdriver

- Hand drill or drill press with countersink bit

- Clamps, ratchet, bar, squeeze. As many as you got

Before committing to a glue up, I **always** recommend with new models a dry assembly. Fit all the pieces together with painter's tape. Take a step back and stare at it. Is this correct? Are you sure?

If everything checks out, I get a pencil and label "Top" or "Inside cabinet" on any pieces that is not symmetrical. Let me give you an example.

Depending on your supplier, your LCD control panel might come in one of two mirrored versions. This is the button input that controls "input" selection, contrast, brightness, and other menu functions with your TFT LCD. The location of this ribbon cable header is something we need to make note of (Figure 5-44).

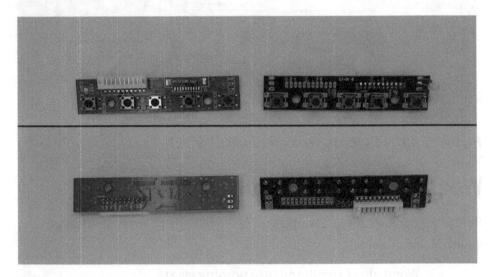

Figure 5-44. *LCD control panel variants*

The cross brace that holds the main LCD bezel has this notch cutout for the cable. It has to be flipped to match this part (Figures 5-45 and 5-46). Once you know the orientation, write it on the panel so you see it during glue up.

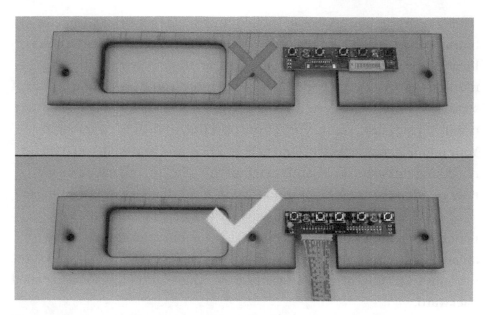

Figure 5-45. *LCD button panel with different ribbon cable connection points*

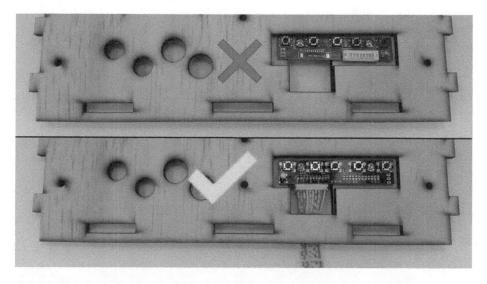

Figure 5-46. *LCD button panel with different ribbon cable connection points, installed into cabinet upper LCD cross brace*

Same precaution applies to your control panel (joystick and arcade button panel). You'd be surprised when you tell yourself, "There's no way I'll glue this backward," and then you do. I get this email every month requesting replacement parts. During assembly, you'll be looking at a lot of standard panels (sights you're familiar with) from a different perspective, usually upside down or mirrored from how they appear in your memory. Your mental tendencies will tend to correct for this, and well, you'll regret not taking that extra 30 seconds to write "this side up" on that panel you now glued backward. Alright seriously this time, that's enough warnings.

Let's assemble. Before we glue any part together, identify the two panels that require countersink holes: those behind the bottom of the arcade (Figure 5-47) and the top control panel piece (Figure 5-48). Be sure to countersink the correct side as these parts have the ability to be installed backward.

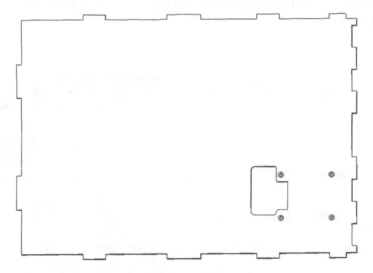

Figure 5-47. *Bottom panel with countersinks*

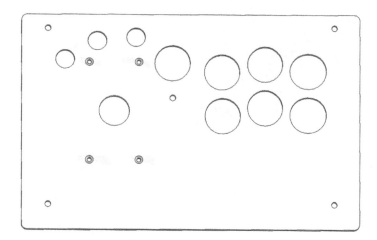

Figure 5-48. *Control panel with countersink*

You can do this later, but countersinking these holes is easier to manage as a single piece and not glued into a larger assembly. Next, take the two cross braces that support the bottom of the monitor bezel and glue them together (Figures 5-49 and 5-50).

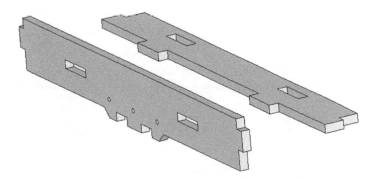

Figure 5-49. *Glue LCD bottom support cross braces*

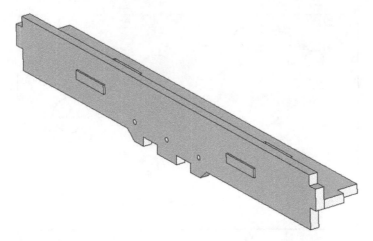

Figure 5-50. *Glued LCD bottom support cross braces*

Glue the bottom of the monitor panel into this cross brace like in Figure 5-51.

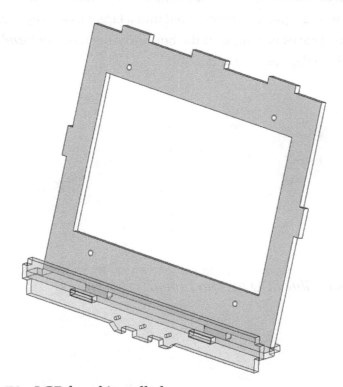

Figure 5-51. *LCD bezel installed*

Add the top cross brace like in Figure 5-52: Remember this piece also mounts the LCD controls like contrast, brightness, and so on. Verify the orientation of the LCD bezel cross brace aligns with the location of your LCD ribbon cable header.

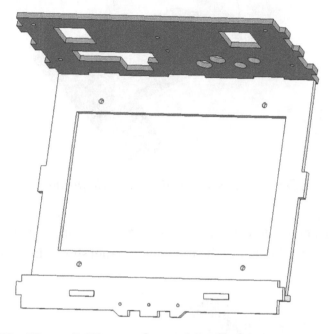

Figure 5-52. *Upper LCD cross brace installed*

Apply glue to the left side of this assembly (Figure 5-53), including the tenons. Insert this assembly into the left arcade panel.

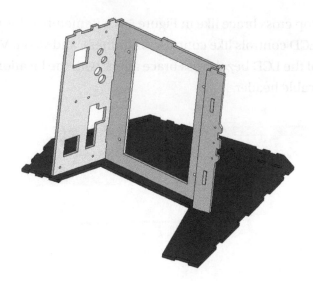

Figure 5-53. *LCD bezel assembly glued to side panel*

This step and the following panel have mortise and tenon joints; they cannot be inserted later. Add the top angled panel shown in Figure 5-54.

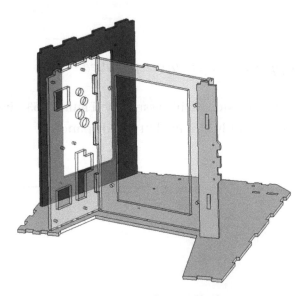

Figure 5-54. *Top-rear access panel installed*

Then add the rear I/O panel (Figure 5-55).

Figure 5-55. *Rear I/O port installed*

Add glue to all exposed sides that contact the side panel. Line up tenons by working from one corner out (Figure 5-56).

Figure 5-56. *Add second side panel*

Add the bottom (Figure 5-57) and make sure the countersink side is facing out.

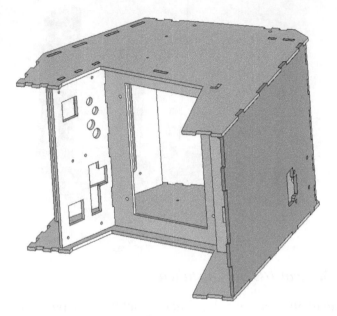

Figure 5-57. *Add bottom panel*

Rotate the assembly upright; position yourself facing the arcade (Figure 5-58).

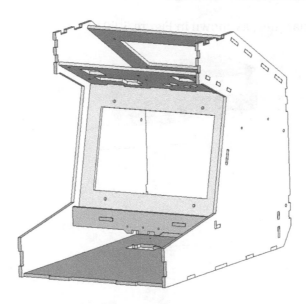

Figure 5-58. *Rotate assembly upright*

Add the top panel like in Figure 5-59.

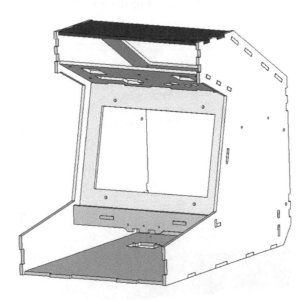

Figure 5-59. *Top panel installed*

And the marquee, as shown in Figure 5-60.

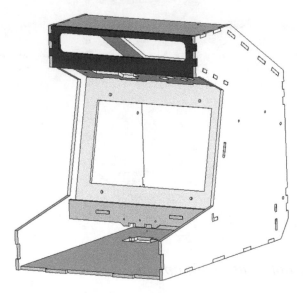

Figure 5-60. *Marquee panel installed*

Add the control panel front cover (Figure 5-61).

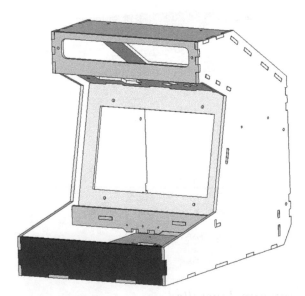

Figure 5-61. *Front bottom control panel installed*

Rotate the assembly so you are looking at the back (Figure 5-62) of the cabinet. Glue on the top rear brace.

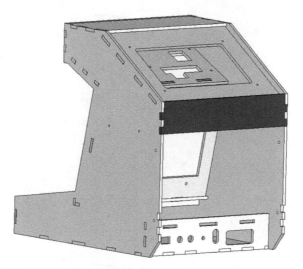

Figure 5-62.   *Rear top brace installed*

Glue the horizontal upper I/O panel (Figure 5-63).

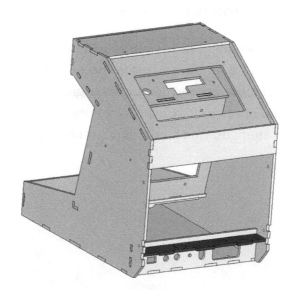

Figure 5-63.   *Horizontal upper I/O panel installed*

Lock this in place with the bottom rear panel (Figure 5-64).

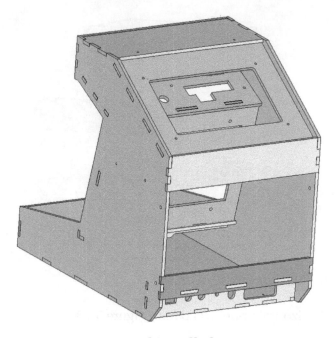

Figure 5-64. *Bottom rear panel installed*

OK! Clamp this assembly like in Figures 5-65 and 5-66. Make sure you're working on a level surface and using spacers between the cabinet's glue joints and your table top. You don't want to glue the cabinet to the table. Using a damp lint-free cloth, wipe off any excess glue. Wait for the glue to cure to full strength. Wait for the glue to cure before moving on.

Figure 5-65. *Glue up with clamps*

Figure 5-66. *Glue up with clamps, second angle*

Be sure to wait for the glue to cure before moving on.

There are few parts left to glue; some are quality-of-life improvements to this arcade and the rest for aesthetic reasons.

Rotate the cabinet like in Figure 5-67, which shows the side view.

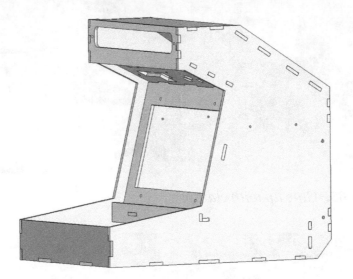

Figure 5-67. *Side view of arcade*

I will make the side panel closest to us transparent (Figure 5-68) to locate the next parts to be glued.

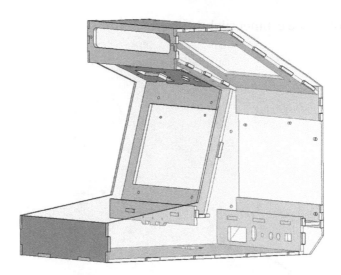

Figure 5-68. *Side of arcade inside view*

The sloping rear-top panel has a large access port (Figure 5-69). The lip that keeps the window from dropping into the cabinet gets glued here. You can use four screw + nuts to keep it in place while the glue dries.

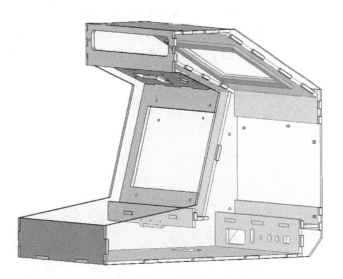

Figure 5-69. *Access port supporting lip panel installed*

Next, rotate the cabinet slightly (Figure 5-70).

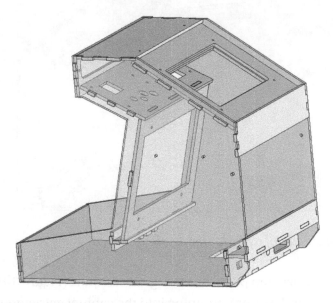

Figure 5-70. *Side view, rear perspective*

Glue the control panel lock to the inside-front of the cabinet (Figure 5-71). If you follow this orientation, then you are planning for the locking control panel with a left-hand joystick setup. This is a traditional joystick configuration.

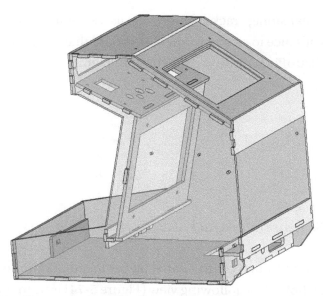

Figure 5-71. *Control panel lock part, inside front*

These parallel strips (Figure 5-72) break up the rear edges and add some more interesting contours to the edges (or I have no idea what I'm talking about). It's an aesthetic thing.

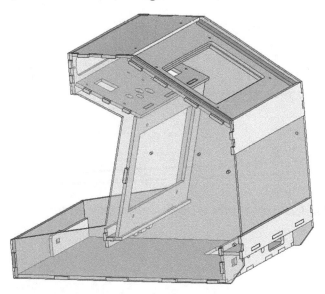

Figure 5-72. *Aesthetic pieces*

Glue this rear storage rack (Figure 5-73) as a separate assembly. It's optional, but it's nice to store a wireless keyboard that gives easy, on-the-fly access to RetroPie's intricate configuration menus.

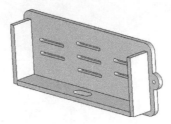

Figure 5-73. *Rear storage rack. Accessorize!*

Grab the two wooden control panel pieces together by lining up the arcade button holes. The following view (Figure 5-74) is from the bottom, or the wiring side. Glue them as shown. Again, this is a left-hand joystick setup. This is a traditional joystick configuration.

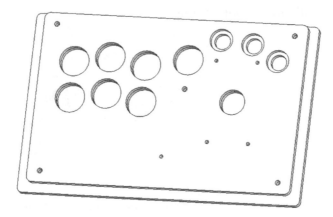

Figure 5-74. *Control panel glued—underside view*

We are at a big stopping point. If you're going to paint the cabinet, this is the time to do so. The cabinet cannot be painted after the all electronics are populated. Let's talk about prefinishing, artwork graphics, and painting next.

Preparing for Painting

Many people comment on how they dislike the finger-joint (puzzle piece) look of the arcade in its current state. I can understand where they are coming from. This design is crucial for a rigid and tough construction, but it is representative of a true arcade. If you want a themed cabinet (Donkey Kong, Pac Man, NeoGeo, etc.), be prepared to spend some time on it.

I prefer the look of proper paint job, color, and good graphics. It's that color scheme, that paint job that triggers all the feels when you look at a machine you're nostalgic for. Painting and the many steps before are where that phrase the last 10% of the job takes 90% of the time rings true. When painting and doing art/graphics, what you get is all in the effort you put in. This is not a job you want to rush or half-ass. Full-ass it and take your time. Expect this to take 2–4 days. Take your time and be patient! Love the paint; be the paint.

Stuff you need for a nice coat of paint

- A powered sander! (This job is too difficult without one)

- Sandpaper for your sander: 80, 120, 220 grits

- Extra sandpaper for manual touch-up (220 grit). Though higher grit would be preferred (say ~500)

- Primer (use a quality primer)

- Foam brush

- Paint (brand name, no cheap stuff or "This half-full can is 6 years old, I'm sure it's fine")

- Wood filler (or Bondo filler/resin)

- Patience

- A place to paint

  - Low humidity, near room temperature, no breezes or wind

  - Well ventilated

Fill all gaps with the wood filler/putty. Use an old gift card to scrape and smooth this over (Figure 5-75). Let it dry. Sand again using 120 grit. It is likely the wood putty will shrink slightly as it dries. You may need to refill sunken holes with the filler. Wait for it to dry and sand again (Figure 5-76).

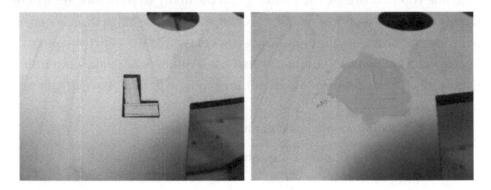

Figure 5-75. *Filling gaps with wood putty*

Follow the directions for your primer of choice. I brushed my prime coat like in Figure 5-77. You can use a spray can primer, but it will take two to three more coats to build the same layers as can paint. On three coats of primer allowing it the dry properly between each coat. This will build up a thickness that we can sand down, removing and filling any gaps and surface inconsistencies.

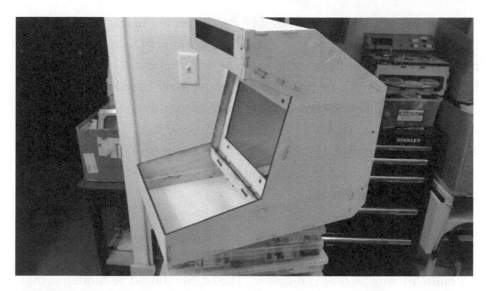

Figure 5-76. *Gaps filled and sanded; pre-prime coat*

Figure 5-77. *First coat of primer*

Be absolutely sure to allow the last coat of primer to dry thoroughly before final sanding. I am using an oil-based primer of a brand name and it goes on thick. You could use a latex-based primer; it is water-based which brings easier cleanup and low odor compared to oil-based primers.

For a smooth surface finish, I find some latex primers are a bit too thick. In the past, I've added Floetrol (a paint conditioner) to thin latex. The Floetrol keeps the paint wet longer which helps the leveling process. Your mileage will vary. You always get better results when you've used paint products a second time.

Bust out your sander again, this time with 120 grit, and sand away the brush strokes. After that, switch to 220 grit and sand the rest by hand. Keep a consistent sanding path to avoid scratches. Wipe all dust away with a dry cloth. Be sure all dust is removed. The seams should be hidden at this point. If they are not, then repeat sanding and priming (Figure 5-78).

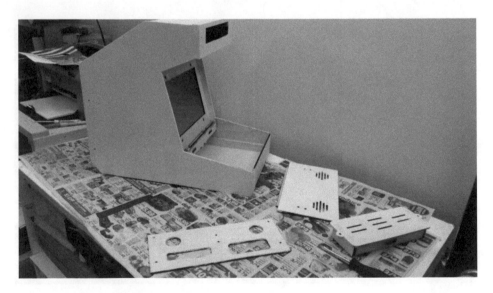

Figure 5-78. *Prime coat done*

I use a quality spray paint for the final coats. Rustoleum in most cases. I prefer spray paint as with a steady hand and ideal painting conditions, it will produce a paint job that usually exceeds expectations. If you have a smooth and good foundation (prime coat), most mid-tier paints will do the job. Following the directions of the paint I used, I did two coats and allowed the paint to dry for 24 hours (Figure 5-79).

Figure 5-79. *Painting where it's convenient*

Then I did a final touch-up with my 220 (500 is better) grit all over. Removed all dust and did two more coats, allowing the last coat 24+ hours to dry before handling. I brought the cabinet out into natural sunlight (on a sunny day) and visually inspected it. I noticed some glossy areas and some flat areas. I decided to do one last coat to even the gloss tones. I let this dry for 24 hours. The final paint job is shown in Figure 5-80.

Note   Follow the paint's directions! If it says let it dry 24 hours between coats, let it dry for 24hrs. Cutting corners here will only result in disappointment and a poor paint job. This is the step that will always show your lack of patience or need to cut corners. Take your time, the effort is worth it.

If you painted your cabinet, the paint must absolutely be 100% dry before moving on. We are going to handle the arcade a lot when adding the vinyl graphics and electronics. If the paint still smells like paint (it's off-gassing), then it's not dry. This can take days. The last thing you want is a fingerprint embedded in that paint job.

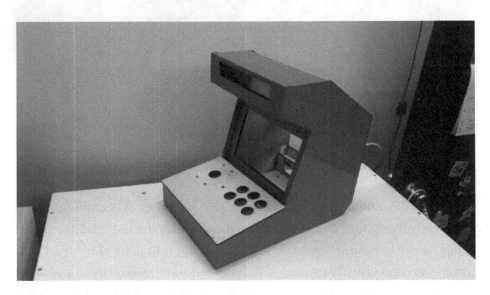

Figure 5-80. *Final paint job complete*

To complete the look, let's add some vinyl graphics to this paint job. Try tracing over some logos and making a vector image. Lay the vectors over the cabinet to get a visual and scale the text to size. This will help you decide if the look is what you want.

Summary

We now have a fully built cabinet with a fancy paint job. If you wanted a display piece for people to notice in your living room, this is perfect. But we want to be able to play games on it, too. In the next chapter, we'll work on hooking up our Pi so that we can play!

CHAPTER 6

Installing the Electronics

Now that the arcade has taken on its proper identity, it's time to install the electronics (LCD, speakers, and amplifier), Raspberry Pi, and connect all to power. I like to start with the LCD, but if you have large hands, I would wait to install the LCD and jump ahead to the subsystems and subassemblies section. The LCD covers up a significant entry point to the inside of the cabinet. If you have trouble working in small spaces, you'll find the following rather similar to decorating a cake inside a dimly lit tissue box.

Installing the LCD

The LCD mounts the same we designed it. Place the four screws into the cabinet, and slide the top and bottom LCD braces into place like in Figure 6-1.

© Mark Frauenfelder and Ryan Bates 2019
M. Frauenfelder and R. Bates, *Raspberry Pi Retro Gaming*,
https://doi.org/10.1007/978-1-4842-5153-9_6

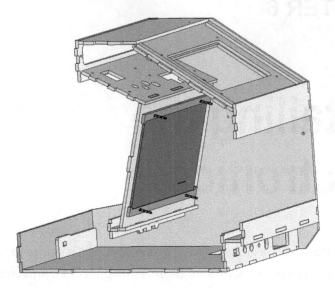

Figure 6-1. *LCD mount installation; top and bottom TFT brackets*

Slide on the plates that hold the LCD TFT in place (Figure 6-2).

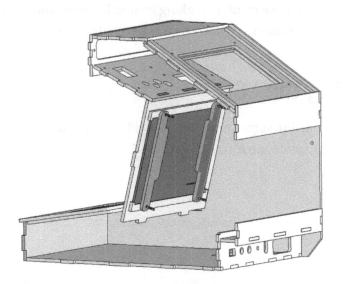

Figure 6-2. *LCD mount with retaining brackets*

Next install the 'H' panel (Figure 6-3), *preferably with LCD's driver board already mounted to it.*

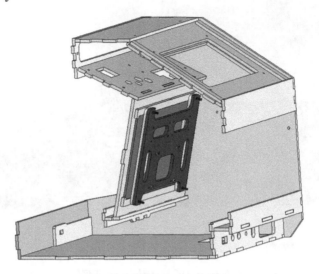

Figure 6-3. *LCD cross brace "H" panel installed*

Attach the ribbon cable from the driver PCB to the TFT panel shown in Figures 6-4 and 6-5.

Figure 6-4. *Back of TFT with LCD driver PCB, note cable connector*

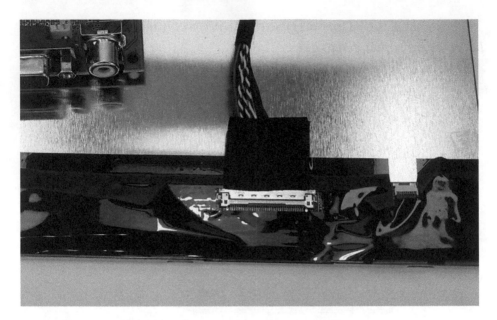

Figure 6-5. *Connected driver PCB cable to TFT*

I use some nylon spacers underneath this PCB (Figure 6-6); the through-hole components have some long legs poking out the bottom; nylon spacers help this board rest comfortably on the wood bracket.

Figure 6-6. *Nylon spacers for LCD driver PCB*

Finish with nuts to complete this subassembly (Figure 6-7).

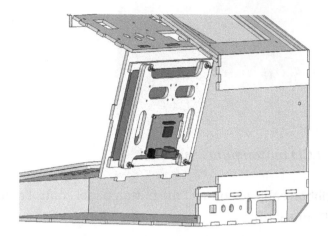

Figure 6-7. *H bracket with LCD driver PCB installed*

Grab the LCD button panel wood piece. Add two spacers (optional) so the PCB rests flat and the through components are lifted off the wood (Figure 6-8).

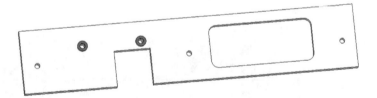

Figure 6-8. *LCD button panel bracket with nylon spacers*

Attach the button PCB with machine screws and nuts like in Figure 6-9.

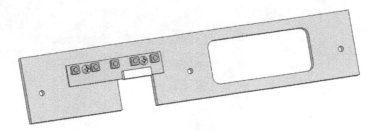

Figure 6-9. *LCD button panel installed*

Use the ribbon cable to connect the button panel control to the LCD driver PCB (Figure 6-10).

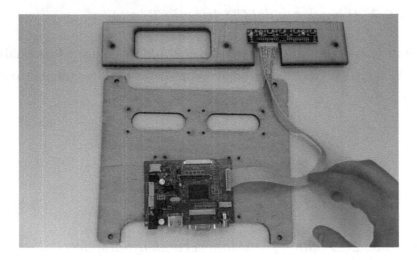

Figure 6-10. *LCD button panel ribbon cable connection to driver board*

The button assembly is mounted with machine screws and nuts as shown in Figure 6-11.

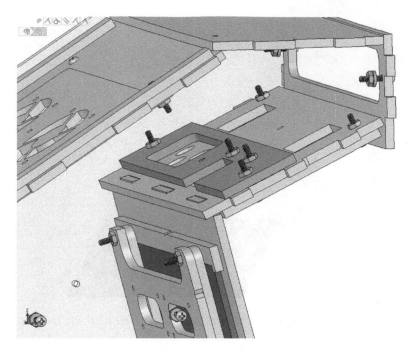

Figure 6-11. *LCD button panel installed inside cabinet; inside view*

This is a good time to install the cover plate for this area—below the marquee where we have a number of buttons. See Figure 6-12 and Figure 6-13.

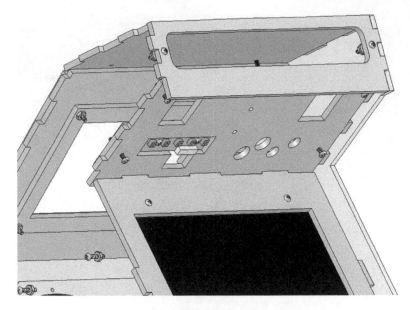

Figure 6-12. *LCD button panel installed inside cabinet; front view*

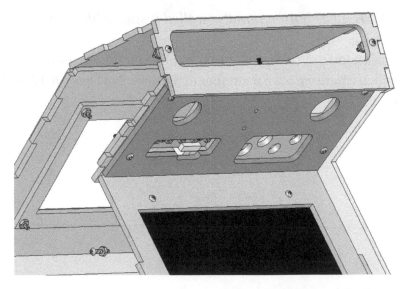

Figure 6-13. *LCD button panel cover (trim) plate installed*

Subsystems and Subassemblies

We've started connecting cables to dedicated PCBs.

From now on, I'm going to use illustrative representatives of some of these components as they are introduced (Figure 6-14). These diagrams show the parts and highlight only the essential ports, headers, and plugs required to wire the arcade.

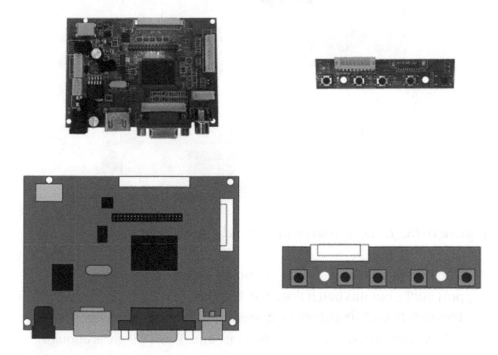

Figure 6-14. *LCD driver and button panel, actual (top) and representative diagram (bottom)*

Figure 6-15 shows what we've connected so far: mainly, only dependent connections in between the LCD, driver panel, and button panel.

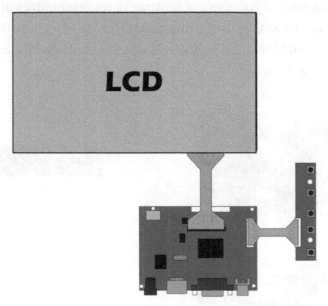

Figure 6-15. *LCD, button panel, and drive PCB connections*

The HDMI-compatible LCD I've chosen is video only. Later versions support audio, but this batch does not. Next is audio.

Figure 6-16 is off-the-shelf 2watt stereo audio amp board. There are many DIY audio amps out there; this is just one. This PCB gives enough audio output to fill a small bedroom (with the right speakers), so this should be plenty for this sized arcade machine. The board also have built-in volume control with buttons and external headers to route volume controls somewhere else.

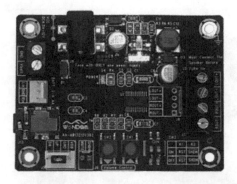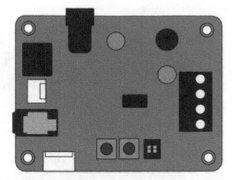

Figure 6-16. *Audio amp (left) and diagram (right)*

Matching speakers is easier when you have narrowed down your amplifier choice. This amp is compatible with speakers that have 4 to 8 ohms impedance. The speakers you select should be midrange speakers (Figure 6-17). This means these speakers can reproduce frequencies in (mostly) the full audio spectrum. Full-range speakers do not perform particularly well compared to dedicated speakers for dedicated low (subwoofer) or high (tweeter) frequencies. But we only have room for one pair of speakers, hence the choice for full range speakers. On this scale, this is our first big sacrifice, but you'll likely won't notice we skipped out on audiophile sound on 8- or 16-bit soundtracks. So, what speaker should we use? As big as possible. I'd pick the largest speaker (in physical size) you can fit in your cabinet. The size is proportional to the volume it can produce. This cabinet can comfortably fit all these sizes shown in Figure 6-18. Pictured are (from left to right) 3″, 2.5″, and 1-inch-diameter full-range speakers. Cheap speakers sound, well, cheap. The speakers pictured are about $4–$6 each or $8–$12. This is defiantly on the low range of things, but far from the bottom of available options. Considering I am not an audio engineer, I'd just be doing high-end audiophile speakers a disservice.

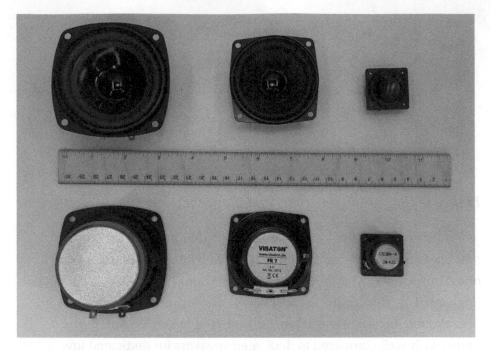

Figure 6-17. *Various speakers for this cabinet size*

The 1 inch speakers will fit underthe marquee as we planned. These 1 inch speakers are for those who insist the speakers should be under the marquee. Figures 6-18 and 6-19 show a cross section of how I mounted these 1 inch speakers.

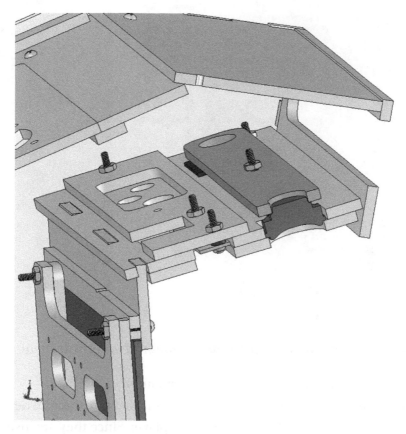

Figure 6-18. *One-inch speaker mount method*

The mounting holes molded into the speaker baffle are ridiculously small; a #2 (~M2) screw doesn't fit, so I opted for the sandwich method. More measuring is involved, but the mount is cleaner and more versatile if you wish to swap these speakers for say LED rings in the same location. (Hint, we'll do that too.) The panel highlighted in green slips over the end of each speaker and retains them by being locked into the control panel with the centered nut and bolt.

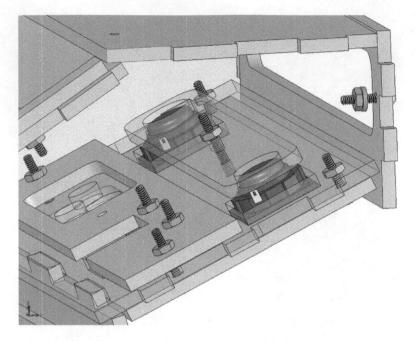

Figure 6-19. *One-inch speaker mount method, alternate view*

But what if you want that larger speaker sound?

The 2.5 and 3″-diameter speakers will fit inside this cabinet. They will face the back of the LCD and project to player. Since they are inside mounted the cabinet body, there will be accidental acoustic properties of our cabinet, both good and bad. Some ranges have a richer, fuller bass sound; other ranges will be a bit muffled. I have other plans for the interior space of this cabinet, so instead of using the 3″ speakers, let's settle on 2.5″. We need to build the subassembly shown in Figures 6-20 and 6-21. This is done by mounting the speakers and amp with machine screws. Don't forget to solder wires of the left and right speakers and connect them to the respective audio amplifier.

Figure 6-20. *Speaker and amp subassembly, rear view*

Figure 6-21. *Speaker and amp subassembly, front view*

Since we are looking at the rear of this speaker subassembly, the stereo left speaker is actually wired to the right (your directional right) output and vice versa (Figure 6-22).

Figure 6-22. *Solder speaker wires*

Don't forget to mount two standoffs on this assembly. These are 1 inch female/female aluminum standoffs shown in Figure 6-23. These will come in handy later when we need an easy way to fasten the rear panel to cabinet.

Figure 6-23. *Aluminum standoffs*

Use the two identical brackets shown in Figure 6-24 and mount the speaker subassembly into the cabinet, but don't actually do it! We still need access to the interior the cabinet, so set this speaker assembly aside for now.

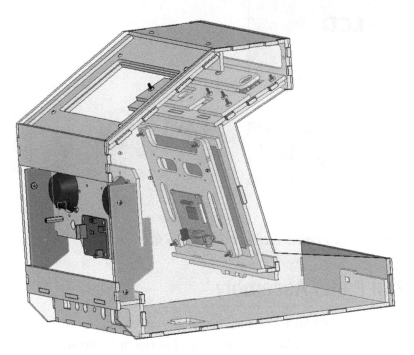

Figure 6-24. *Mount speaker subassembly with brackets*

Updating our connection diagram brings us to Figure 6-25.

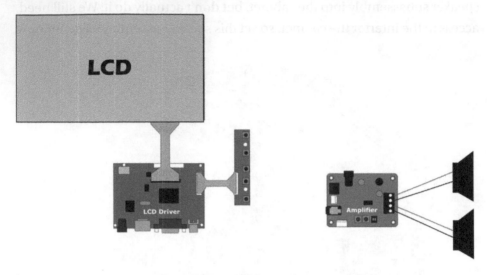

Figure 6-25. *LCD and speaker wiring so far*

Control Panel Assembly

It's time to assemble and wire the control panel for our arcade. There are two routes we can take with the control panel in conjunction with the Raspberry Pi. Because the Raspberry Pi has GPIO pins, we could use some software to poll the GPIO pins and interpret button presses and joystick inputs as keyboard inputs. The other route (and more universal) is using a keyboard encoder. The keyboard encoder is exactly as it sounds; it takes discrete inputs and encodes them to keyboard signals. You press a button, and the Raspberry Pi (or any PC that accepts USB HID devices) see a keyboard key activated. This is simple and essential component to build large-scale Multiple Arcade Machine Emulator (MAME) cabinets. It's also my recommended way for MAMES with two or more players. I prefer keyboard encoders for single-player RPi cabinets too; that's more because many of these encoders include wiring harnesses and I hate wiring. We will look at each approach.

In either regard, we need to populate our control panel and assemble the layers. First, mount the joystick (Figure 6-26) with flat head screws and split washers to keep the nuts secure during heavy use.

Figure 6-26.   *Control panel with joystick, bottom view*

If you printed, cut it out and place it on the top of the control panel. Place the clear acrylic over and fasten with the binding posts (Figure 6-27).

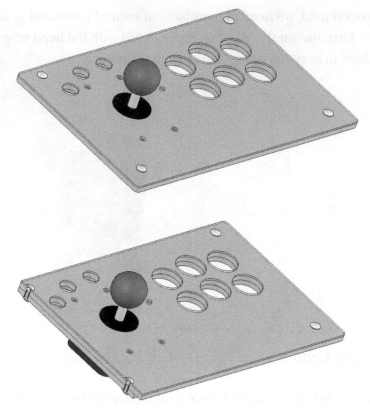

Figure 6-27. *Control panel assembly with binding posts*

Insert your buttons of choice. I'm using some smaller general-purpose push button above the arcade to save not just space but cost. You should have something like Figure 6-28 or 6-29 now.

Figure 6-28. *Assembled control panel, no artwork*

You can place the joystick dust cover (the flat, black plastic disk) on now and screw on the ball top if you like.

Figure 6-29. *Assembled control panel with artwork layer*

Flip the control panel over; now it's time to wire each input to the keyboard encoder, pictured in Figure 6-30. If you bought your encoder on eBay, hopefully (and usually) it came with a wiring harness.

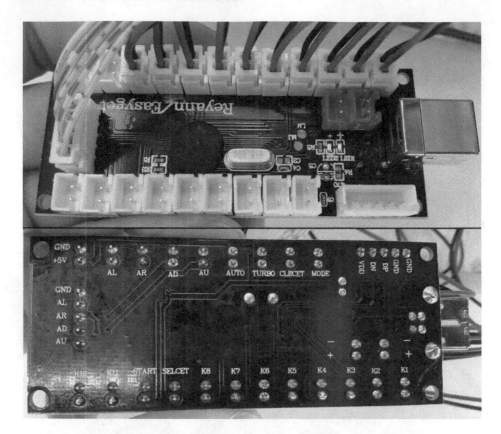

Figure 6-30. *Generic keyboard encoder top and bottom of PCB*

This takes all the pain out of a rather tedious and repetitive task.
Figure 6-31 shows a fully wired control panel. Each button gets a wire pair
and plugs into its respective place on the encoder. More arcade keyboard
encoders will have some generic wiring labels (button 1, button 2, or K1,
K2, K3 in our example) to guide you.

Figure 6-31. *Wired control panel underside with a keyboard encoder PCB*

Note the USB type B female connector on this keyboard encoder. The included USB cable will connect the encoder to your Raspberry Pi (Figure 6-32).

Figure 6-32. *Wired keyboard encoder with USB cable*

We haven't installed the Raspberry Pi into the cabinet yet and for good reason. Another option for implementing arcade controls is done by wiring directly to the Pi's GPIO headers. It's best to do this with easy access to the Pi, before it's mounted into the cabinet.

The extra software you need is Adafruit's Retrogame found here at their github repository: https://github.com/adafruit/Adafruit-Retrogame

I recommend following the associated instructions from Adafruit: https://learn.adafruit.com/retro-gaming-with-raspberry-pi

Installation can exist on top of any RetroPie; install with the following script:

```
cd
curl https://raw.githubusercontent.com/adafruit/Raspberry-Pi-
Installer-Scripts/master/retrogame.sh >retrogame.sh
sudo bash retrogame.sh
```

Adafruit's Retrogame utility can be configured with a *config* file located:

```
/boot/retrogame.cfg
```

Because this file exists in/boot, you can edit it easily: either locally on the Pi or remotely via SSH.

The configuration file maps whatever you have connected to useable GPIO pins and simulates keyboard keys as buttons are closed, triggering GPIO pins low. Within the config file, you can assign GPIO pins and what corresponding keyboard key is triggered. Table 6-1 is an example sort-of-universal-for-most-emulators config file I use. It reads as Keyboard KEY | GPIO pin#| Arcade Input.

Table 6-1. *Retrogame one-fits-most sample configuration*

Keyboard KEY	GPIO pin #	Arcade Input
UP	2	Joypad Up
DOWN	3	Joypad Down
LEFT	4	Joypad Left
RIGHT	17	Joypad Right
A	22	"A" button
B	27	"B" button
X	23	"X" button
Y	24	"Y" button
F1	8	"Menu" button for retroarch
RIGHTSHIFT	10	"Select" button (Console)
ENTER	9	"Start" button (Console)
1	18	"Start 1P" button (MAME)
ESC	7	"Escape" key to exit ROM
R	11	"R" button
L	25	"L" button

Wiring the joystick and buttons inputs to the RPi is simple since no pull-up resistor or additional hardware is needed. It is a tedious task to wire ten buttons with four directional inputs, all with a duplicate path that returns to ground. There is something we can do to assist with what goes where.

I've wired this before, hundreds of times. And I despise it. So, to ease the pain, I've got a few pro-tips or quality-of-life improvements. We've already settled on a button/keyboard mapping as defined in the example config file. Trust me, you want to settle on something before continuing.

We are going to make another cheat sheet! Just like the one in Chapter 6, but instead of GPIO numbers, we just put the intended arcade controls on the sheet. See Figure 6-33.

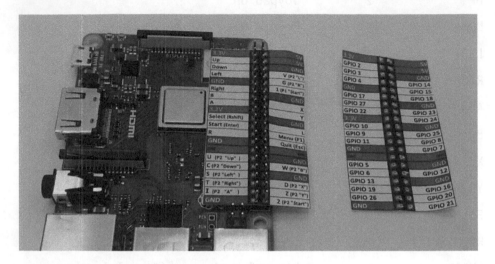

Figure 6-33. *GPIO cheat sheet for arcade inputs*

Print this out to scale and smash it onto the RPi's GPIO headers. Now we don't need to go back and forth translating what button input is assigned to what GPIO pin. Following the cheat sheet, the "Start" button is wired like in Figure 6-34.

Figure 6-34. *Arcade connections to GPIO headers; Start button wired*

Just repeat the signal and ground wire connection for the rest of your buttons and joystick inputs. Speaking of joystick inputs, this is another one of those mirrored image brain teasers. If you're looking at the bottom of your Sanwa joystick (you likely are at this step), the directional inputs are arranged like in Figure 6-35.

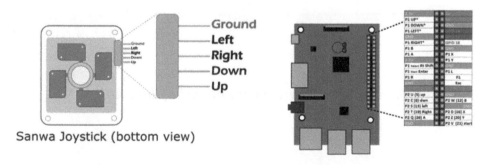

Figure 6-35. *Joystick and GPIO input labels*

I usually transcribe this in pencil on the underside of the control panel as I'm wiring. Basically, do as much prep work in advance to avoid wiring something wrong. This is usually (it will happen to you) where a wiring issue will arise.

Keeping with the unfortunate theme of wiring diagrams, if you wire all your arcade inputs to the RPi, it'll look something like Figure 6-36, but with fewer straight lines. If you are a messy point-to-point wirer, rest assured! We'll just stuff that mess away in the cabinet to definitely not have to troubleshoot later. My button layout is just that, my button layout. If you want to move placements around or enable hotkeys, do so! Please take some time to stare at this diagram. It's very helpful and also took too much to draw.

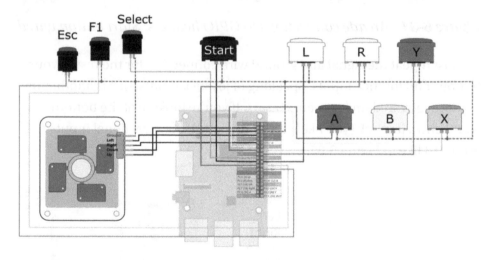

Figure 6-36. *Raspberry Pi arcade input wiring diagram*

Note The button labels in Figure 6-36 are not only a general emulator/console mapping but also the literal keyboard keys they trigger. The exceptions are Enter and Right Shift; these trigger "Start" and "Select", respectively. The "x button = x key", "a button = a key" idea was to not confuse myself. This scheme has caused me some, but not a lot of confusion in hindsight.

You've either got no wires connected to your RPi right now (you're using a keyboard encoder) or a pile of spaghetti poking sticking out of the Pi's GPIOs. Either way, the control panel is complete. This is a great time to mount the Pi into the arcade. Place the control panel into the arcade and add the locking bar like in Figure 6-37.

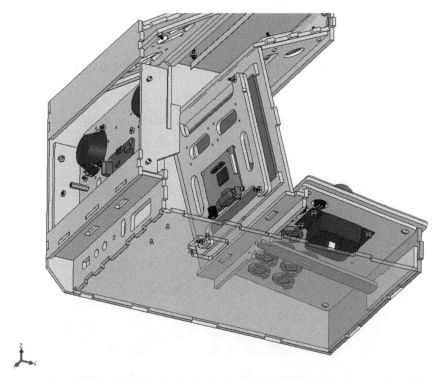

Figure 6-37. *Underside, control panel lock bracket*

Add two screws into the rear of the control panel cross brace, and loop a rubber band over these around the control panel locking bar (Figure 6-38). I still have not drawn a rubber band here.

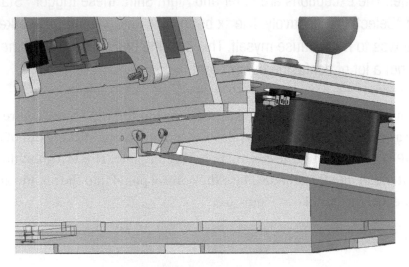

Figure 6-38. *Rubber band that I don't know how to draw to lock the control bar*

This will keep the locking bar in position. Place the long screw through the top of the control panel; fasten with a thumb or nut (Figure 6-39).

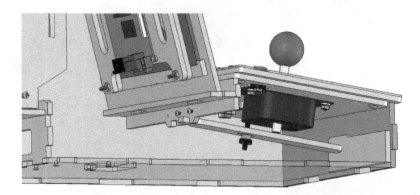

Figure 6-39. *Thumb screw to lock control panel into cabinet*

Next, focus to the rear of the cabinet (Figure 6-40).

Figure 6-40. *Side, before mounting Raspberry Pi*

Add the Raspberry Pi riser plate along with four mounting screws (Figure 6-41).

Figure 6-41. *Riser plate for Raspberry Pi*

Add nylon spacers (optional) so pressure is transferred into the RPi PCB and not the through components protruding under the RPi. Mount the Pi, add nylon spacers, and fasten with nuts (Figure 6-42).

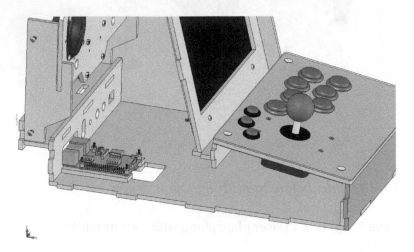

Figure 6-42. *Mounted Raspberry Pi*

With the integration of the main control panel, we need to populate and wire the remaining buttons in the cabinet. Figure 6-43 shows some extra hardware needed.

Figure 6-43. *New switches and buttons. From left to right: 5.5x2.1mm DC barrel jack, latching on/off switch, latching button (green), and momentary button with LED (red)*

Figure 6-44 shows where we add some extra function buttons under the marquee, two of which we will use for amplifier's volume up and volume down. The remaining two will be latching switches, of which are placeholders for optional features later on.

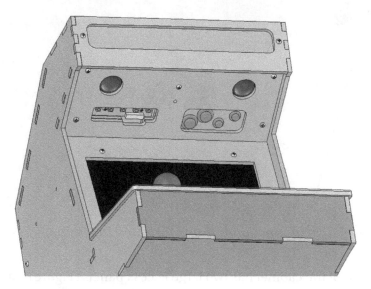

Figure 6-44. *Added function buttons under marquee*

First solder wires to the buttons and switch contacts. Feed the wire into the mounting hole followed by the attached buttons and switches (Figure 6-45). Attach the plastic retaining washer from the inside.

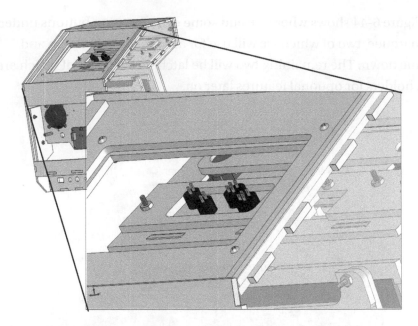

Figure 6-45. *Extra function buttons installed in cabinet*

The rear of the cabinet has two large access panels (Figure 6-46) to help us wrangle these wires.

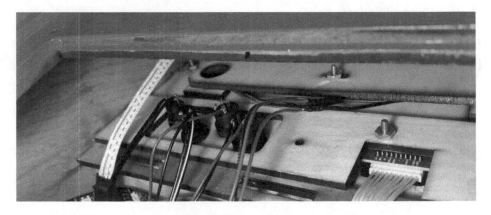

Figure 6-46. *Inside cabinet with wired extra function buttons*

The volume buttons are wired like in Figure 6-47, giving us volume control from the front of the cabinet.

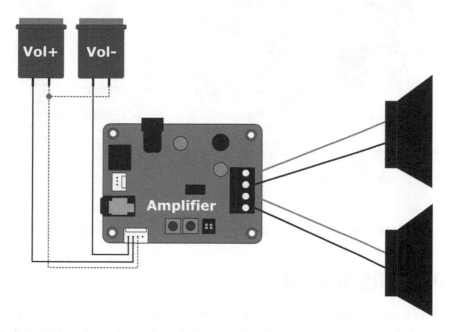

Figure 6-47. *Speakers, amplifier, and volume button wiring diagram*

With the rest of the hardware placed in the cabinet along with the appropriate controls (on/off switches) installed like in Figure 6-48, it's time to wire power. These switches will control power, the backlight marquee lights. On the rear of the panel, we also mount the DC input jack, where main power enters the cabinet.

There's a lot to talk about in the next steps, so new heading!

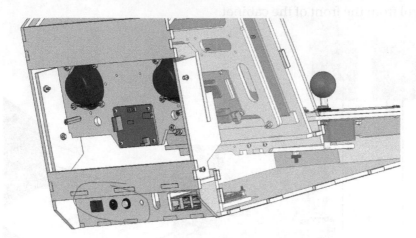

Figure 6-48. *Power switch, input power connection, and switch*

Powering Wiring

The section is most likely the most complicated part in the arcade build. The task ahead has a lot of details within it, and if you're unfamiliar with basic electronics, it's like you could be following a guide with no intuition of right or wrong. The room for error is high due to the number of wiring connections, and the margin for error is even higher for those unfamiliar with circuit basics. Because this task is complicated and laborious, I've tried to simplify it for myself because I've had to wire many mini arcade cabinets. I made this custom PCB (Figure 6-49) that does two things: First it distributes power and routes all power terminations to screw terminals. This makes for easy integration of on/off switches and provides simple connections to various components of an arcade (Figure 6-50).

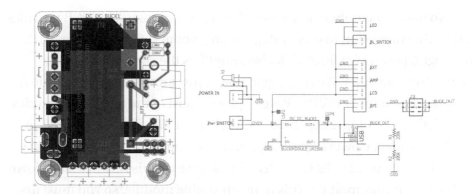

Figure 6-49. *Ryan's custom Power Block Arcade PCB, for wiring mini arcade machines. Pictured left is PCB; right is schematic*

This makes for easy integration of on/off switches and provides simple connections to various components of an arcade (Figure 6-50).

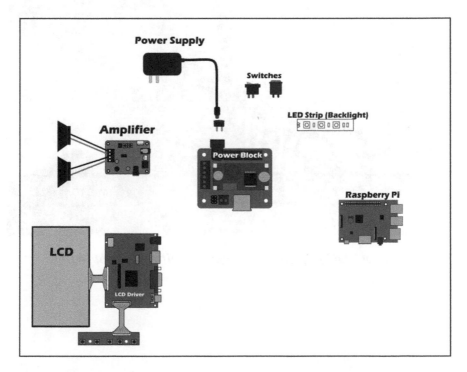

Figure 6-50. *Arcade electronics and switches we need to wire*

245

No need for cumbersome wire splitting and routing. This PCB provides a straight connection to every integral component (LCD, amplifier, LED backlight, power switch, etc.). It also simplifies the connection of the step-down converter. We're going to power this arcade off of one single AC adapter that outputs 12VDC. We can power most of the arcade electronics at 12V; that's including the amplifier, backlight LEDs for the marquee, and the LCD screen. However, the Raspberry Pi cannot take 12 volts. We have to step down this 12 volts to 5 volts. The way we do this is with a step-down or buck converter module. This is an adjustable module, so you must first power it with the input voltage and connect a voltage meter to the output. Using the adjustable trim pot in our step-down (buck) converter (Figure 6-51), turn this until the output is around 5.15volts (Figure 6-52).

Figure 6-51. *DC-DC step-down converter with trim pot being adjusted*

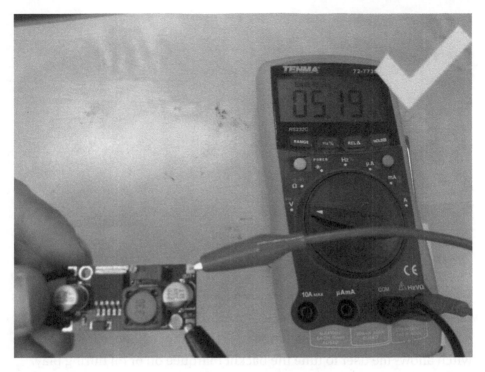

Figure 6-52. *DC-DC step-down converter adjust to output 5.2 volts*

The Power Block Arcade PCB integrates the buck converter with simple terminal connections for the other arcade components. First we're going to center around that PCB which I've shown in Figure 6-53 assembled with buck converter and related hardware.

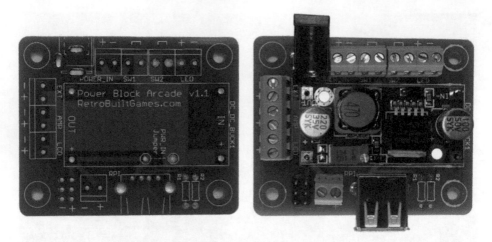

Figure 6-53. *Power Block Arcade PCB; bare PCB (left), assembled (right)*

The big picture is shown in Figure 6-54 with all the critical components wired into the central power block (if removed from the cabinet shell). The rocker switch controls the main power to the entire arcade, while the green switch allows the user to tune the backlit marquee on or off during play.

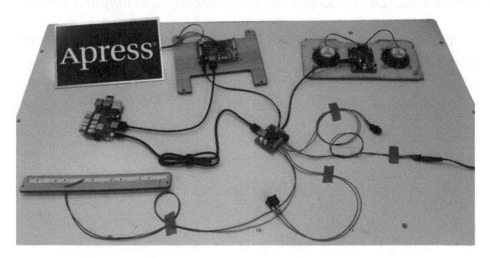

Figure 6-54. *Overview of all electronics wired without the cabinet*

Figure 6-55 illustrates how to wire this together.

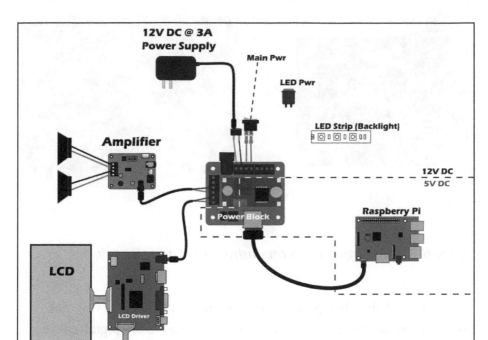

Figure 6-55. *Basic power connections to electronics: Raspberry Pi, LCD, audio amp, and input power supply*

Fortunately, most of the hardware I've selected is OEM and is manufactured with the intent for modular installs. The amplifier and LCD driver panel have DC input jacks for power (Figure 6-56).

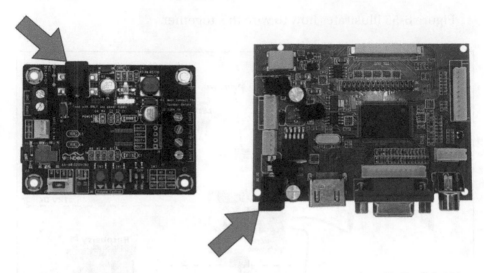

Figure 6-56. *DC input jacks on audio amp and LCD driver boards*

Another off-the-shelf part courtesy of the CCTV industry will make connecting power the custom PCB simple; we'll use a DC pigtail cable (Figure 6-57).

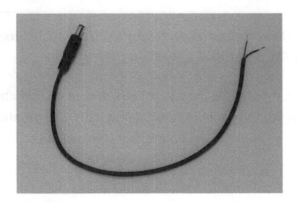

Figure 6-57. *DC pigtail*

Just make sure to verify the polarity is correct before supplying power. All these parts pictured require center-positive barrel jack connectors. That means the center of the DC plug is positive and the outer sleeve is negative (ground actually). You likely have seen this before on the end of your AC-DC power supply (Figure 6-58) without knowing what it means.

Figure 6-58. *A 12 volt, 3 ampere power supply with center-positive barrel end*

What's in a Quality Part?

Now is a great time to mention our main power supply feeding the arcade cabinet. It is generic in branding; however, it does retain some notable features:

- Outputs 12VDC @ 3A (enough power for this arcade without pushing our power supply to it's limits).

- Plug is center-positive (pretty common, somewhat standard in 12V DC power supplies).

- UL listed *with the file number* (passed some rigorous testing; implies a quality power supply; we can probably trust the three ampere rating).

- Long cord= very convenient.

There are many generic 12V power supplies. The aforementioned characteristics are ones to lookout for. In particular, we need enough current to power all our electronic components; 2amps is about what the arcade consumes, but picking a supply that outputs 2 amps wouldn't give us any headroom. Any cheap supply (non-UL listed) might be able to meet a 2 amp continuous draw, but for how long before failure? Give yourself a safety factor of 50%. The power supply will have a longer lifespan and provide a more stable output if its normal operation is not bordering its specified output limits.

Our power supply is UL listed. A lot of generic supply might use the Underwriters Laboratories (UL) insignia falsely to be more marketable or appear "safe." We can actually search this file number on UL's web site (Figure 6-59) and see UL listed corroborating records.

Figure 6-59. *UL listed power supply record*

And there it is, the model number and manufacture. This all checks out fine. If we explore more, like the UL standard this power supply was tested against, we can identify what the intended use of this power supply is. A few clicks and links later, we find the standard: UL 6500: Standard for Audio/Video and Musical Instrument Apparatus for Household, Commercial, and Similar General Use. Even better. If you had $1,635, you could purchase a digital copy of this standard and determine what safety features the power supply might contain (over current, thermal shutdown, short-circuit protection) and what tests it passed to become UL listed (electric shock, resistance to fire, impact/drop testing, etc.).

That was sort of a sidebar, but it's a quick glimpse into what separates quality electronics from everything else. It's the largest contributor to cost too. One thing to note is, just because this arcade is connected to a UL listed power supply does not dictate the rest of the arcade can adopt the same pedigree. Just because the power supply is "safe" *does not mean* everything downstream is also safe.

Connect an HDMI Cable

Remember our wiring diagram? Here's an updated diagram; Figure 6-60 illustrates power wiring up to this point.

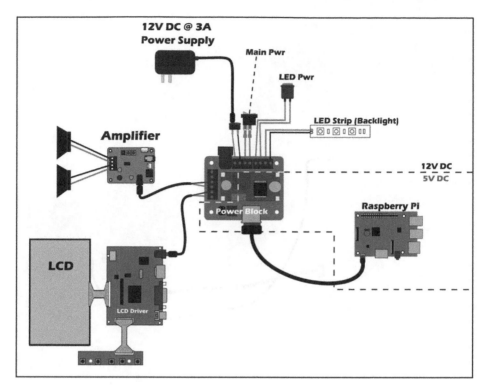

Figure 6-60. *LED strip with on/off button wired into cabinet*

We are missing some audio and video connections. Connect an HDMI cable (1 ft preferably) between the RPi and the LCD driver. We also need a 3.5mm stereo audio cable between the RPi and the audio amp like in Figure 6-61.

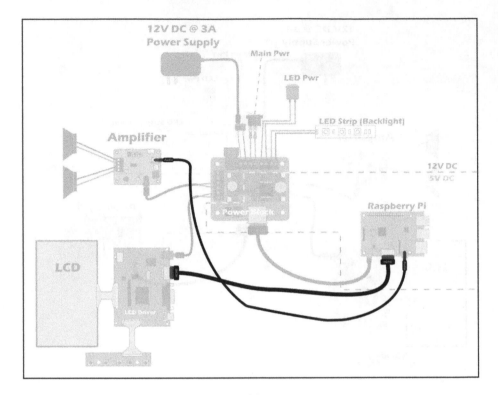

Figure 6-61. *HDMI and audio cable connections*

Ground Loop Fixes in Audio

Before we power on the arcade, I'm going to add a fix to a problem that might be present in this, and many other DIY arcades. We are using analog audio and have an unintentionally ground loop. Our setup has an unintentional ground loop. We made two return paths for ground: one between the amplifier ground and the Raspberry Pi's DC power ground. The power-plane ground and the audio ground have the same reference and share a path. You can see this path or loop highlighted in Figure 6-62. This means the return to ground power path can travel through our audio ground and cause some unwanted audio noise and interference.

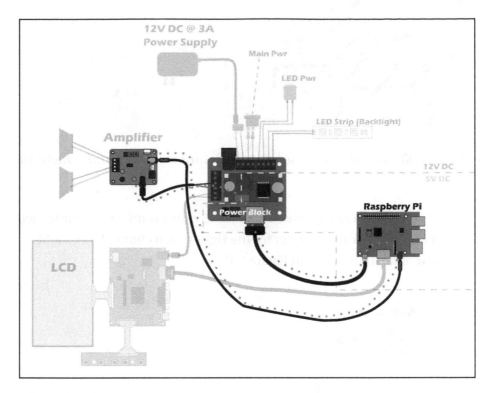

Figure 6-62. *Ground loop path*

To fix this, we need to isolate the audio signal ground or break the electrical continuity in analog ground. Since audio is analog, we can use a transformer to isolate the audio path which breaks the DC ground path but still lets analog signals pass through. We do this with two small transformers. In comes another custom PCB (Figure 6-63). This ground loop isolator.

257

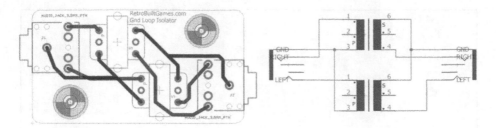

Figure 6-63. *Ground loop isolator PCB diagram (left) and schematic (right)*

It is merely two analog stereo audio jacks with a transformer for the left channel and another transformer for the right stereo channel. Let's add that to our audio line shown in Figure 6-64.

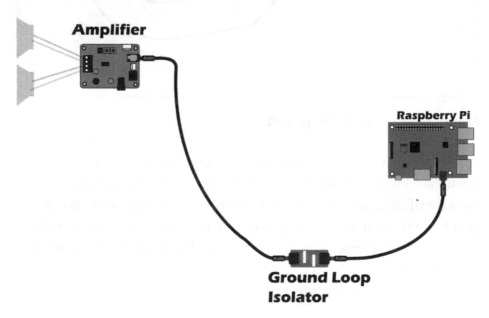

Figure 6-64. *Ground loop isolator in line with Raspberry Pi and audio amplifier*

This audio abnormality is common in systems with two different power references. Let's say you're listening to music on your phone or MP3 player through a physical connection to your car stereo's auxiliary jack (before Bluetooth was standard). If you plug your phone or MP3 player's charging cable while listening to music, you might hear a hum or buzz in the audio. This is another scenario where a ground loop occurs. The fix is the same. You can easily buy a ground loop isolator for about $8, but it's only $1.20 in parts, so why not make it? We've gone this far building the arcade, what's one more custom part?

Buttoning Up

Nothing else to do but close up the arcade! I went the extra length to design an internal shelf for storage for an extra controller for player two or the power supply when not in use. Let's bolt in the side brackets and install the shelf like in Figure 6-65.

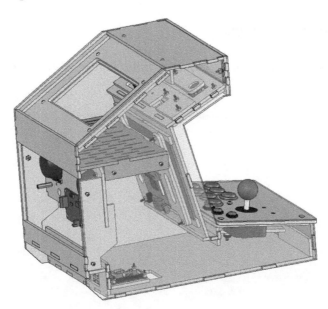

Figure 6-65. *Internal shelf for storage*

Speaking of storage and unnecessary parts, I also made a small bracket that bolts onto the rear panel (Figure 6-66). This gives some space for a wireless keyboard or other accessories.

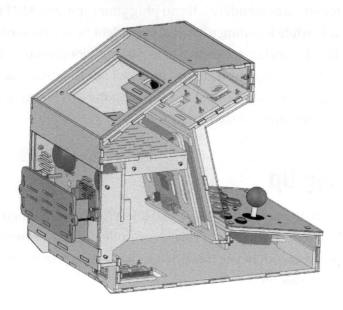

Figure 6-66. *Rear storage*

Now fasten the rear panel with two bolts (Figures 6-67 and 6-68).

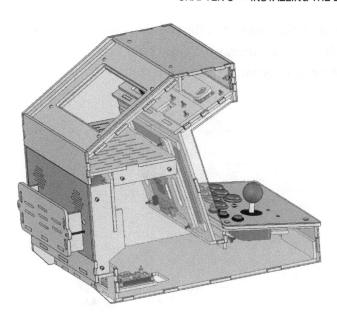

Figure 6-67. *Rear panel*

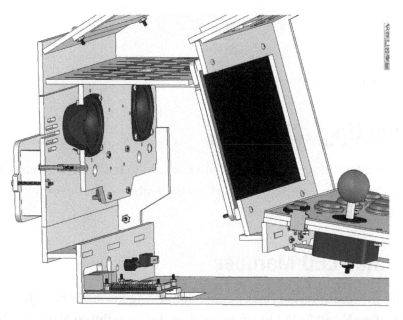

Figure 6-68. *Bolt connection to fasten the rear panel to the speaker bracket subassembly*

Remember bolts connect to the standoffs mounted into the speaker subassembly. See the cutaway in Figure 6-68.

Add the top access panel (Figure 6-69).

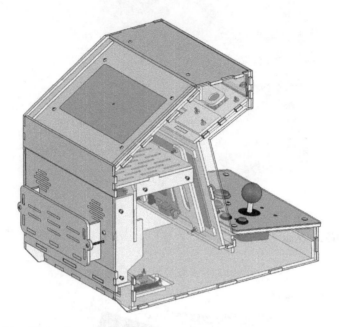

Figure 6-69. *Top access panel*

Bonus Upgrades

There are a few little extra touches you can add to really make your cabinet pop. In the next few steps, I outline how to go above and beyond for a few little extra cool bonus features.

Animated LED Marquee

First off, the marquee gets an upgrade. Replacing the static backlit graphic panel is an 8x48 LED matrix driven by an Arduino Nano inside. Figures 6-70 and 6-71 show the 8x48 LED matrix segment fitted to a mounting panel and driven with a custom Arduino clone board (not in the arcade). The individual 8x8 matrix segments are MAX7219-based modules, easily found on eBay (about $4 for a series of four connected matrices).

Figure 6-70. *LED matrix in bright light*

Figure 6-71. *LED matrix in low light*

The required Arduino libraries to drive them are MD_Parola and MD_MAX72XX. A future project for me is to drive them with the Raspberry Pi and write a script that scrapes the ROM name currently loaded and pushes the string to the marquee. Someday.

Battery Powered

I mentioned in Chapter 5's Design Review, this arcade is small enough to make it battery-powered. Let's give that a try! After all, we have the room and planned for this: the larger cabinet size and the internal storage shelf. I have some Ryobi power tools I use at home, so let's see if we can utilize a battery pack readily available, the cordless Ryobi battery in Figure 6-72. This can be any drill battery you have or any battery pack that outputs at least 12V.

Figure 6-72. Cordless drill battery pack to make a portable mini arcade

I rebuilt the inner shelf as a power regular with a custom step-down converter. Since the drill battery is 18v (nominal), we need to step the voltage down to the input power we design the arcade electronics to run off, 12v.

The rebuilt inner shelf shown in Figure 6-73 has a custom 3D printed bracket (Figure 6-74) that contacts the battery's + and – terminals when inserted. With this battery, I get about 2.5 hours of run time; that's with normal screen brightness and medium sound volume.

Figure 6-73. *Battery power regulation shelf*

Figure 6-74. *Pictured center, custom 3D printed battery clip to interface with battery packs*

The battery voltage, which varies from 20v to 16V (from fresh to dead charge) is regulated and passed to the arcade. You can see the current voltage of the battery pack in Figure 6-75. I have plans to make a battery level indicator on the outside, rather than having to peak at the number to determine when the battery is near empty charge.

Figure 6-75. *Mini arcade running off a drill battery*

Neo Pixel LED Lighting

My last modification features some Neo Pixel LEDS that add some multicolor glow to the arcade (Figure 6-76). These Neo Pixels are individually addressable, so each LED's color can be assigned in a stip.

Figure 6-76. *Neo Pixel LEDs inside arcade for some flare*

The extra buttons below the marquee toggle if these LEDs are on or off; since now that we have battery power, we want the ability to turn off nonessential features when playing the arcade. With the top access panel in place (Figure 6-77), this gives a dark room a soft glow from the inside LEDs.

Figure 6-77. *Glow from interior LEDs*

Finally, remember our design used the 2.5 inch speakers mounted behind the LCD? I demonstrated how to mount 1 inch speakers below the marquee, but in the end we did not install them. So, what did I do with that space? The same mounting principles applies, but this time I mounted some Neo Pixel LED rings (Figure 6-78).

Figure 6-78. *Neo Pixel "Jewel"*

You might have noticed a multicolored glow earlier; this is the Neo Pixel ring (Figure 6-79).

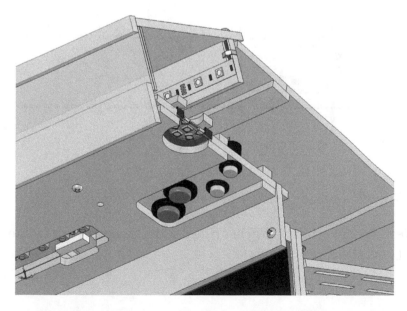

Figure 6-79. *Mounting a Neo Pixel cluster below the marquee*

Keyboard for a Joystick

Retro arcade games work great on arcade joysticks. But what if your fancy
is more PC-based? Some retro PC shooters emulated on DOS box perhaps?
Compared to a keyboard, an arcade joystick does not have the same feel
when playing 1990's First Person Shooters. Let's replace that joystick with
a keyboard PCB! First, the custom PCB design in Figure 6-80. I'll refer to
this as a key-stick because I can't think of anything better to call it. I'm still
experimenting with the idea at this time.

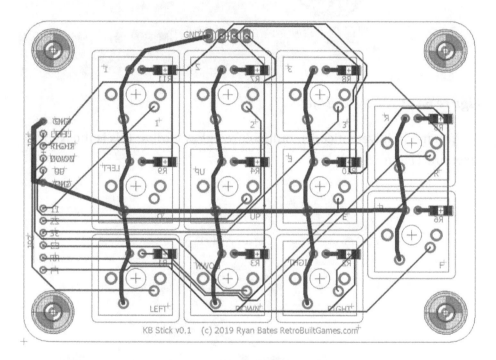

Figure 6-80. *Keyboard-joystick PCB, first revision*

Next, solder keyboard switches (Cherry MX of course) and resistors for
3mm LEDS in Figure 6-81.

Figure 6-81. *Rear view of key-stick, soldering resistors*

Though optional, you can't call yourself a gamer unless you have backlight mechanical keyboard keys (professionals have RGB backlit keys). Refer to Figures 6-82 and 6-83 for LED installation and backlight testing. Why red LEDs? It's what I had. Why orange keycaps? Again, it's what I had. I didn't plan for this very well.

Figure 6-82. *Solder LEDs to PCB*

Figure 6-83. *Add keycaps to key-stick*

You might notice two "Esc" keys. The keycap sample packs I bought only have so many unique keys. Let's just call it a place holder for now.

The control panel requires an overhaul. I wanted to avoid this looking like a drop in number pad, so I'm only using eight keys plus two offsets. Figure 6-84 shows the rear view of the control panel. This is mounted the same way, with four flat head screws.

Figure 6-84. *Control panel (rear-view) to mount key-stick*

Note the two pencil lines. To make this key-stick a nontrivial hardware swap, I wanted the main arrow keys to match the exact same order of the Sanwa-JFL joystick. The arrow keys are wired as such on the PCB. To facilitate that easy swap, the interface needs to match; male 0.1" headers are the choice. I have a right-angle header sticking out of the key-stick in the same fashion as the Sanwa joystick earlier. The pencil line in Figure 6-84 indicates where this header is soldered to the PCB. The header is through-hole and protrudes out of the PCB—same side that needs to mount under the control panel. I have to mill out some wood with a rotary tool; otherwise, the key-stick will not sit flush on the control panel. Figure 6-85 shows the routed channels.

Figure 6-85. *Routed channel to make way for soldered PCB headers*

Finished product is shown in Figure 6-86. I think I will move the keypad up about an inch. My wrist could use some more room when using this keypad.

Figure 6-86. *Key-stick prototype control panel with Doom theme*

I'm pretty happy with the key-stick as a concept. I just wanted to showcase some ideas that can motivate your arcade to something very custom. You can still incorporate the traditional trackball setup too, but never be afraid to experiment.

Don't think the custom PCBs are a cost-prohibited accessory. If you ever need to design and layout a custom PCB, try Eagle CAD, KiCAD, or EasyEDA. Getting custom and professional PCBs are surprisingly cheap. These PCBs were about $0.50 plus shipping. Seeed Studio, JLB PCB, and PCBway are cheap, low-quantity manufacturers great for prototype circuit boards.

Summary

Thanks for reading and following along. If it was your first introduction to arcade building and you're feeling a bit overwhelmed, don't worry! The best place to start is anywhere, as long as you start. Do not be concerned about the end result, you can only be accountable for the work you're doing now—focus on the task at hand. Every arcade you build, your skills will increase. The next arcade you build will reflect this. I've been building for a long time.

The next chapter will focus on a two-player arcade design, a sort-of hybrid to the mini arcade (not portable, but transportable) and on a scale that's a bit more practical for extended play.

CHAPTER 7

Build a Desktop RetroPie Arcade

In previous chapters, we covered some significant milestones when building an arcade. On any arcade scale, we've talked about specific arcade hardware, methods of fixturing, and electronic component selection. Those methods will carry over to a larger scale. The larger scale also inherits some bonuses: as the cabinet expands in size, we gain some flexibility. A larger cabinet provides some much needed interior space. This build will have a bit more room regarding how to mount components and integrate electronics. If anything, this build doesn't involve working in cramped spaces. I will be covering build topics a bit more broadly if they've already been discussed in the previous chapter. Previously, we built a 1:8 scale arcade.

In this chapter, we will build a 1:3 scale arcade. This is probably the fan favorite size for a few reasons: The screen size is standard; the control panel fits two people comfortably (arcade games are a social activity). Another feature focuses on nostalgia. The arcade body is large enough to immediately be recognizable. You see it and know just what it is. The 1:3 scale is also the limit to being transportable. It's still moveable for one person and can be hidden away if not used for long periods of time (haha, we had a laugh there didn't we?). The 1:3 scale desktop arcade is the ultimate compromise in your relationship when your partner says "you're not putting that in here, are you?"

© Mark Frauenfelder and Ryan Bates 2019
M. Frauenfelder and R. Bates, *Raspberry Pi Retro Gaming*,
https://doi.org/10.1007/978-1-4842-5153-9_7

Monitor Selection

Like with any arcade design, we again need to plan around the most critical component—the monitor. Fortunately for us we are now at the scale where we can be thrifty and parts are plentiful. Modern computer monitors are very inexpensive, and LCDs from 10 years ago are pretty much worthless nowadays. They can be found at thrift stores, yard sales, and dumpsters. If you don't want to buy a used LCD (or even a new monitor) for this project, be resourceful. Many large businesses, universities, and schools upgrade their computer equipment every 5 or so years. Make a contact from the inside, preferably within the IT department or seek out an e-cycle (electronic recycling) company. With any luck, you'll hopefully find a cheap PC monitor destined for the landfill that will work as a cornerstone for an arcade cabinet.

I've selected something extremely common from the early 2000's era. Fortunately for us, this era was before the adoption of widescreen monitors, so we have a LCD aspect ratio that is close to a 4:3 ratio. This monitor happens to be 5:4 ratio and is a good candidate for an arcade monitor. Today's yard sale special is a 17 inch Dell 1704FPTt seen in Figure 7-1. When picking a monitor, try to get one with DVI. This will give us the least amount of headache when interfacing with the Raspberry Pi's HDMI video out. It's not likely you'll find a 4:3 or 5:4 ratio monitor with HDMI from this era, but that's not a total loss. HDMI is built from the DVI standard; the most we'll need is a cable (HDMI to DVI-D) which are under $5 shipped on eBay.

Figure 7-1. *Generic 17" Dell monitor*

Monitor Teardown and Measuring

Before we can design a cabinet around this monitor, we need to do some preparation, well, mainly just a tear down. Start by removing the stand so we just have the LCD assembly like in Figure 7-2.

Figure 7-2. *Monitor with stand removed*

The hard part here is removing the plastic bezel or frame. Though this step is not vital, it is required for that professional look of our arcade cabinet. You might have noticed some DIY arcades look like they were built around a PC monitor and others look like they were designed with OEM LCD panels in mind, showcasing a clean and almost seamless fixturing of the LCD TFT to the arcade body. Nothing exudes "DI-whY" when you see "Dell" at the bottom of the screen while playing PacMan. These things aren't authentic to the arcade experience. It's not wrong, it just lacks polish. We are going for the professional look; therefore we need to get to the raw TFT.

The plastic shell of this monitor is bulky and would position the TFT behind the bezel, making an unsightly gap between the two. Another reason, inherent to this Dell monitor, is it has no VESA mounting holes, so mounting it by any traditional means is difficult. If we want to mount the monitor around the TFT perimeter like in the previous build, the smooth contoured shell exterior makes this near impossible. We need to remove the plastic shell and expose the LCD TFT assembly. Find some flat tip screwdrivers and poke around the seams of this plastic shell. Figure 7-3 shows us getting somewhere. As you pry the bezel trim seams apart and work around the edges, wedge in pennies or guitar picks to keep the shells from locking back together.

Figure 7-3. *Remove the monitor's plastic shell*

Once you get the shell removed, usually in two halves, remove any unnecessary mounting hardware attached to the LCD metal body. Note the uniform and plain square metal body in Figure 7-4. This is the LCD subassembly. Before it's branded by say Dell or HP, this is the raw OEM assembly with the power supply and TFT driver circuitry, just what we need and nothing more. Be very mindful of the front control panel and it's fragile ribbon cable. These monitor controls like power, contrast, brightness, and input are still vital to the monitor function. Just be careful not to break this small control panel PCB or tear the ribbon cable.

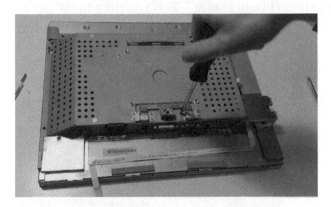

Figure 7-4. *Remove any extra stand hardware*

We are nearing the point of no return. Flip the monitor over and power it on. Verify the buttons function, the monitor turns on and displays a clear image over the DVI port. If you haven't destroyed the monitor, then good!

If you haven't done this yet, we need to verify one critical feature for this arcade. We need to make sure when the monitor is on, that it will still stay on when power is removed and reapplied. Meaning, if the monitor is displaying an image (there is an input source present) and you remove the power cable and plug it back in, the monitor will return to an ON state and display the last input source. Conversely, if you have to press the power button on the monitor to get a picture after power loss or power cycle, this not a deal breaker. It just becomes a very annoying step every time you turn on the arcade to also press the monitor's power button. Remember the monitor power button is on this ribbon cable. Our plan is to tuck this button panel out of sight in the back of the arcade's owner access panel. Most notable branded PC monitors remember their power button state on power cycle, but not *all*. Since this monitor remembers its power state, we can tuck this control panel out of sight. Don't scrap it! We'll just hide it somewhere in the back of the cabinet.

Your monitor still works; you didn't put a giant scratch in it with those screw drivers? Good. Does it remember its power state and the button panel still functions like in Figure 7-5? If yes, then great! Let's move on and measure the monitor's overall width, view window, and thickness.

Figure 7-5. *Final test of the raw TFT assembly*

I'm going to measure everything in mm since I have a metric tape measure and frankly base 10 numbers make sensible measurements than fractions. This monitor was likely made in a metric standard country, so we're more likely to get round mm dimensions anyway. This monitor measures to be 362mm wide by 298mm tall as shown in Figure 7-6.

Figure 7-6. *Monitor TFT assembly dimensions*

The viewable area is 340mm x 273mm, confirming the 5:4 (1.25) ratio ($\dfrac{340mm}{273mm} = 1.24$). The bezel is a nice round 10mm and 12mm at the sides and top/bottom areas. Now we can transfer this to CAD and layout the monitor bezel and overall size of the arcade (Figure 7-7).

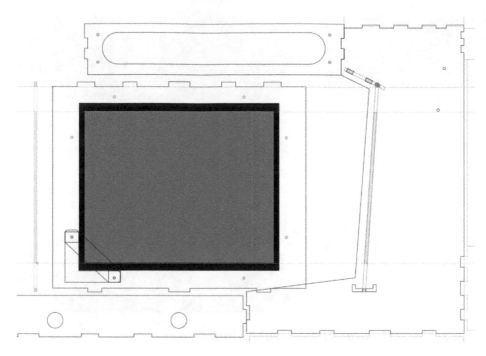

Figure 7-7. *Layout to mount LCD and overall arcade size planning*

Recall if you want to stick to drawing the entire cabinet in 2D like in Figure 7-7, you need to draw the monitor in at least two perspectives: The front view and the side view of what is shown. Hence the horizontal layout lines that span across the drawing. This helps me figure out the monitor's position from a side view and plan the respective brackets that mate with each other.

To mount this monitor, I am just going to cradle it from all four corners.

This is the simplest method possible to mount the monitor. It is also the mot direct. This method requires accurate (+/- 1mm tolerance) measurements of the monitor assembly. To make sure the metal bezel of the monitor is hidden, I will shrink the LCD cutout on the arcade bezel by about 2mm in both directions. This means my arcade's LCD cutout is just undersized of the monitors view screen. This will accommodate any shift from the bolt mounts, and if my measurements are off just slightly, we won't see the monitor's metal frame (hopefully). Always leave room for the fudge factor. The mount method is shown in CAD in Figure 7-8.

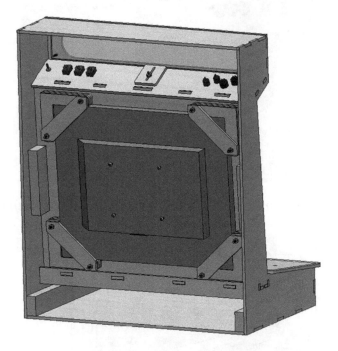

Figure 7-8. *Monitor mounting method, rear view*

A cutaway view is shown in Figures 7-9 and 7-10 for extra clarity. The method is the same, we are building up the same flat part to make a bracket equal to the thickness of the monitor. It's then sandwiched or braced in all four corners. The square and flat edges of this TFT assembly make this relatively simple as long as your measurements are accurate.

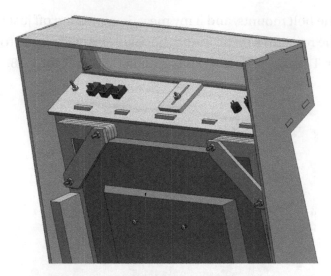

Figure 7-9. *Monitor mounting method, rear view close-up of bracket*

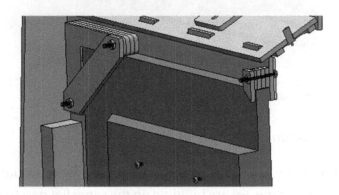

Figure 7-10. *Monitor mounting method, rear view side cut away*

The size of this 17 inch monitor determines the size of the arcade body with a few restrictions. We are stuck with a pretty plain body size (Figure 7-11), but we are balancing the limits of a midrange laser cutter for this sized project.

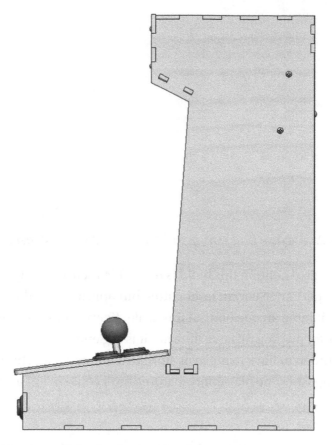

Figure 7-11. *Arcade body design for this monitor*

The laser cutting I'm using has a maximum cutting area of 28 x 18 inches, so some sacrifices have to be made. Extra flourishes in the body design are forgone, so the biggest parts of this cabinet can fit on a standard sheet size (Figure 7-12); that being 24 x 16 inches. I've already cut all my stock wood to 24 x 16 inches (this size generally fits the smallest laser cutters I have access to), so this design is sized to these limitations.

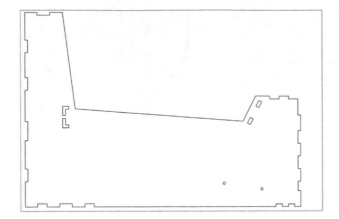

Figure 7-12. *Arcade body on my biggest sheet size for laser cutter*

I should also mention this build is using 1/4 inch-thick plywood, pretty doable for a midrange 80watt laser cutter, but approaching the limits for a sturdy and durable arcade body at this scale. Keep in mind some quality-of-life goals for owning this machine are it is big enough to be enjoyed, but not a burden to have to move or store when not in use. This shallow body accomplishes the playability features but keeps weight and bulk at a minimum.

Desktop Arcade Features

The cabinet I've designed is illustrated in Figure 7-13.

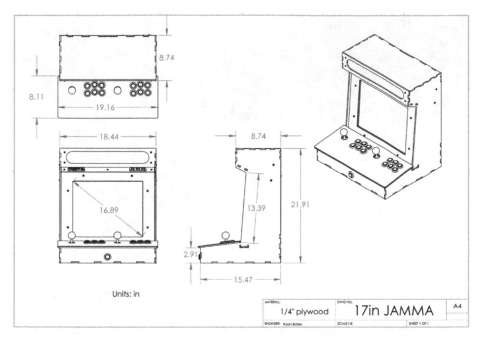

Figure 7-13. *Desktop arcade design for 17 inch PC monitor*

We are working on a larger scale, so some access and design solutions need to be considered and resolved:

- Access to Raspberry Pi (cannot be under the arcade like previous cabinet design)

  - USB, Ethernet ports, and SD card access

- AC power into cabinet. LCD needs 120V AC

- Heat management inside cabinet; ventilation fan needed?

Let's explore some of those solutions. First, the Raspberry Pi's mounting location. I want the floor of the cabinet body to house what will probably be a power strip for 120V AC. This means it's likely to have big power adapters and cables cluttering up the floor of the arcade. That is no place for the exposed Raspberry Pi. I've chosen to mount the Pi to the back panel of the cabinet, with a cutout to access the SD card, and another cutout to access the USB and Ethernet ports (Figure 7-14).

289

Figure 7-14. *Raspberry Pi cutouts for ports and SD card access*

With our larger monitor, it's best to feed 120V AC into the arcade so there is direct access to 120V. We need a modular way to feed power into the arcade and switch it on and off. I went with a very standard IEC power socket, and an illuminated 120V Double Pole Single Throw (DPST) switch seen in Figure 7-15.

Figure 7-15. *Power input and switch locations*

Make note: The input power plug connection should be located closer to the middle of the cabinet. The switch should be toward the edge of the cabinet. When facing the cabinet and reaching around to turn it on, the switch should be closer to your hand. These details are important to the user, not the builder. We are both, so lucky us.

Our monitor might be out of its shell, but the heat dissipation inside the cabinet may still be a concern. To mitigate this, the rear access panel of the arcade have a 120mm fan installed (Figure 7-16). I removed this fan and finger guard from a dead PC power supply. Recycled monitor and PC power supply; yes, we are working on a budget.

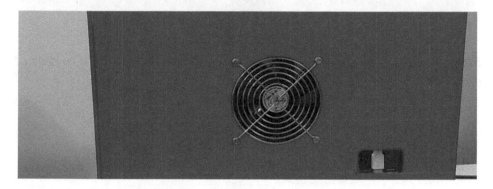

Figure 7-16. *Fan for airflow (heat removal)*

As it turns out, this monitor is pretty generic. Removing the branded shell exposed the metal casing which fortunately has a standard VESA mount built in. This simple 100x100mm mount will also give us a method to mount and organize some of the internal wiring. Again, the floor of the cabinet will be left open for bulky power cables and AC outlets. The theme here is to separate the AC and DC wiring. I cut a rectangular piece of wood with a VESA mount pattern in the middle. Figure 7-17 forecasts how wood panel will be used to mount our Arcade Power Block PCB, a ground loop isolator, and provide place to fix the monitor's display controls (shown just taped, but you could hot glue it).

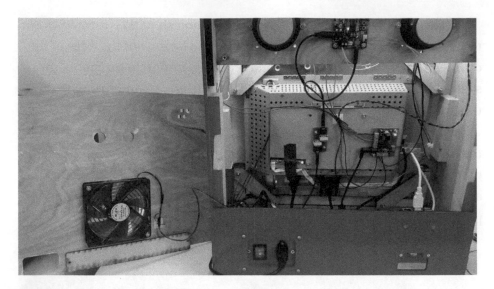

Figure 7-17. *Preview of internal wiring with plate mounted to rear of monitor*

Designing the rest of the cabinet panels gives us this cut layout shown in Figure 7-18.

Wood

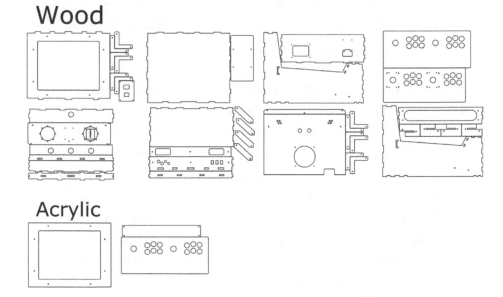

Acrylic

Figure 7-18. *Desktop arcade cut layout*

One big benefit of putting so much time in our CAD file aside from knowing things will fit correctly is the low material cost to cut this arcade. If we nest out parts like in Figure 7-19, everything still fits on one standard 8x4ft 1/4 inch plywood sheet with plenty left over. That makes the raw material of the body between $12 and $30 depending on the plywood quality. We can build an arcade shell for under $30. Ignore the fact that the tool to cut this is $25k. That's what we call unnecessary details. You can absolutely simplify this design. Remove the finger joints and cut this cabinet using more tradition woodworking tools.

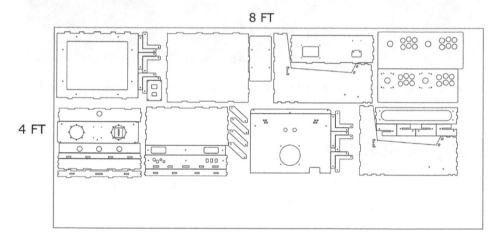

Figure 7-19. *Arcade body on one standard plywood sheet*

With the amount of linear cuts in this design, we're still clocking in at about 45minutes of laser cutting time (using an 80watt machine). Keep this in mind if you outsource the design and are paying for either laser run time or the cumulative length of cuts.

Before we assemble, we need just a bit of extra wood hardware, some 1 x 2 inch common lumber. Figure 7-20 shows some strips of pine ($3 for 6ft). We'll need this for assembly, best to have it now. To cut this, you'll need a handsaw or jigsaw. A circular saw is even better; a miter saw is best.

Figure 7-20. *Common board lumber; 1 x 2 inch pine strips needed cabinet strength*

Body Assembly

Assembly begins with gluing the monitor bezel with the bottom cross brace set as shown in Figure 7-21.

Figure 7-21. *Monitor bottom cross brace set*

294

Glue the monitor bezel and top brace (Figure 7-22).

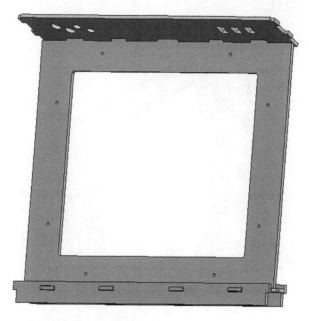

Figure 7-22. *Monitor bezel with bottom and top cross brace*

Flip this assembly on its side and glue to the interior of the cabinet side panel (Figure 7-23).

Figure 7-23. *Add arcade side panel to monitor bezel assembly*

Glue the opposite side panel on (Figure 7-24) then flip the cabinet upright.

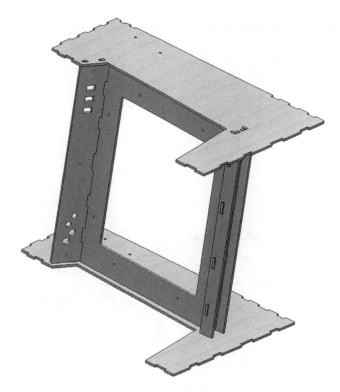

Figure 7-24. *Add opposite side panel*

Glue the arcade bottom and rear I/O panel (Figure 7-25).

Figure 7-25. *Add arcade bottom and rear I/O panel*

Add the front panel to the arcade (Figure 7-26). This panel can be modified to have as many buttons as you need. For this design, I have chosen just one arcade button for the front panel. Your design might vary. This single button will act like a "shift" key essentially doubling the buttons (function wise) on the player control panel. I'll explain more about this in a later section.

Figure 7-26. *Front panel with one hole*

Continue assembling the arcade by adding the marquee panel and the top rear back panel (Figure 7-27).

Figure 7-27. *Add the marquee panel and the top rear back panel*

Glue the top panel on (Figure 7-28), completing the body shell.

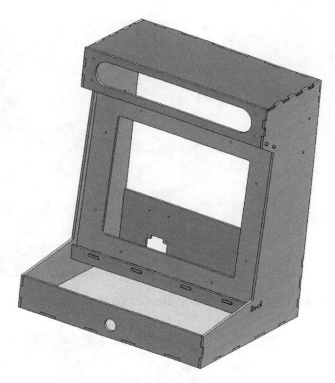

Figure 7-28. *Glue top panel to complete arcade shell*

Clamp this shell assembly together like in Figure 7-29. If you're like me and only have so many clamps, you might need to glue the cabinet in sections. Wait for the glue to cure before gluing the next panel sections on (Figure 7-30). Though I don't recommend the glue-by-section method, I also don't recommend buying a bunch of clamps that you might not use again.

Figure 7-29. *First glue and clamp up using limited clamps*

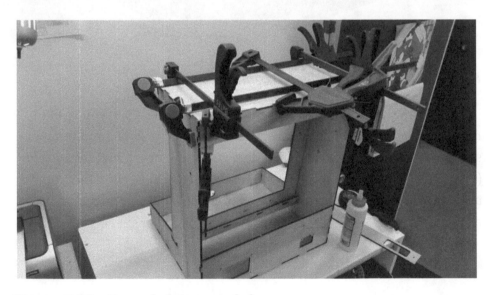

Figure 7-30. *Second glue up and clamp*

Wait for the glue to cure before moving on.

Reinforce Cabinet Body

This shell is not very sturdy for the weight of the monitor it needs to hold. The finished weight of the cabinet is around 30 lbs. I plan to take this arcade to shows and conventions. It will be in the back of an SUV for road travel. The frame gets stressed significantly. We need to add some bones to reinforce the structure, hence the common board we have on hand. This can be any scrap wood in strips, but if you don't have a table saw to rip some straight strips, any common dimensional lumber or trim will work. Cut this common board into strips like in Figure 7-31. These strips will fit inside the arcade corners, adding some needed strength to the cabinet.

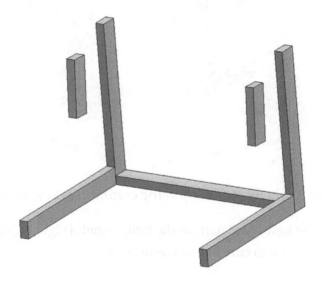

Figure 7-31. *Bones to strengthen the arcade body*

I've glued these reinforcing strips into the arcade like in the x-ray view of Figure 7-32.

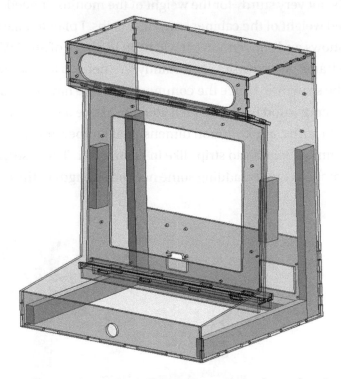

Figure 7-32. *X-ray view of reinforcing common board strips*

Clamp these new wood parts to the body panels (Figures 7-33 and 7-34) and wait for the glue to cure before continuing.

Figure 7-33. *Reinforcing common board clamping part 1*

Figure 7-34. *Reinforcing common board clamping part 2*

Sand, Paint, Repeat

With the cabinet body complete, the next probable step is painting. I mean this is the best time to do it. Let's review the finishing process (Figure 7-35).

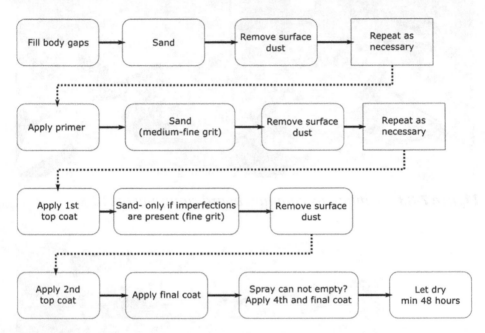

Figure 7-35. *Process for a good paint job*

Expect to spend a few days here. Fill in any gaps with paintable body filler or Bondo. Sand the excess smooth. Apply a prime coat to the entire body (Figure 7-36).

Figure 7-36. *Prime coat after body filler and sanding*

Once the prime coat is dry, sand the entire area with 220 grit and apply a second coat of primer. You're now ready for the top coat of paint. This arcade is a bit larger, so while I have the limited opportunity, I'm going to paint this in a paint booth (Figure 7-37). A paint or sometimes call spray booth is a climate-controlled painting booth, with three out of four walls meant for getting messy. The rear wall is a large mesh filter that continually pulls a large value of air to remove airborne paint particulates and exhaust paint vapors. This booth also helps dry paint faster with a constant current of clean air circulating past the drying paint. Apply your top coat like in Figure 7-38.

Figure 7-37. *Cabinet inside paint booth; ready for top coat*

A paint booth is not necessary, but it's a big convenience. I apply four spray top coats of paint, allowing about 10 minutes between each coat.

Figure 7-38. *First layer top coat applied to cabinet*

To recap, the filling sanding and priming steps will take the longest time commitment. Don't rush the paint process. Mistakes or rushed steps will show in the finish. Take your time; follow the paint's directions. Let the paint fully dry before continuing. I typically use spray paint. If it is all tacky to the touch, the paint is still drying. Another method I used, if I move the painted part into a small room, within a few hours, the room smells like paint—it's not dry yet. The paint is still off-gassing. Let it dry. The last thing you want is an embedded greasy fingerprint in your paint job.

With paint out of the way and completely dry (at least 2–3 days), let's begin assembling the cabinet with the electronic components.

Mounting the Monitor

This is one of those "if you have a friend to lend an extra hand" sort of steps. If you haven't already done so, glue the bracket pieces together (Figure 7-39) so they match the monitor's thickness. Each stack is usually 3 to 3.5 pieces. This stack happens to be 3.5 layers. You can get the half stack from cutting 1/8in-thick plywood instead of 1/4in. You should have four bracket stacks. Set these aside, we'll need them in a few minutes.

Figure 7-39. *Glue the monitor bracket pieces to make a bracket*

The monitor bezel artwork layer needs to go in next. This gets sandwiched with the clear acrylic layer on top. See Figure 7-40 for a side view cutaway of the layers. To fit the theme of this arcade, I'm going to make the bezel black. You could paint the bezel area black. However, I always found acrylic on top of paint weird. The highs and lows of a painted surface are emphasized when you press clear glass or plastic on top. Hence I prefer some artwork layer in this scenario.

Figure 7-40. *Side cutaway of bezel layers. Acrylic top layer is noted. Artwork sits under this layer*

Laser cut the bezel interior with black poster board paper (Figure 7-41). This poster board goes under the acrylic later. A craft knife can also make this. The black poster board creates a consistent and matte surface. Uniform and nondistracting is a great choice for a bezel.

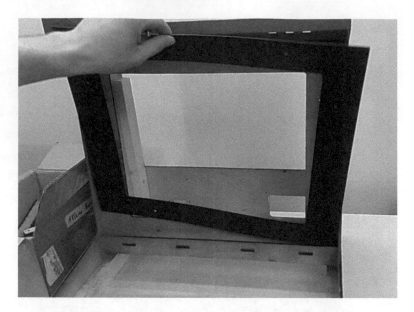

Figure 7-41. *Poster board for bezel artwork layer*

The monitor's weight and size is awkward since you need one hand for the monitor and the other to fasten a nut, all the while hoping the bolts don't back out of the frame. The best way to do this solo is fasten the bottom brackets with the diagonal braces using 1.75″ bolts. (These are #8-32 bolts; M4x40mm would also be fine.) Add the top brackets with the bolts, but set the nuts and two cross braces aside *within reach*. Refer to Figure 7-42.

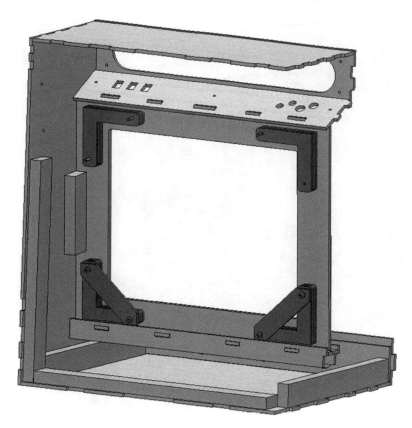

Figure 7-42. *Attach brackets*

Place the monitor in (Figure 7-43) and hold it in place with one hand. With the other hand, add the cross braces and nuts to lock the monitor into position (Figure 7-44). If your bolts back out, just start over. You can use masking tape on the front to keep the bolts from backing out.

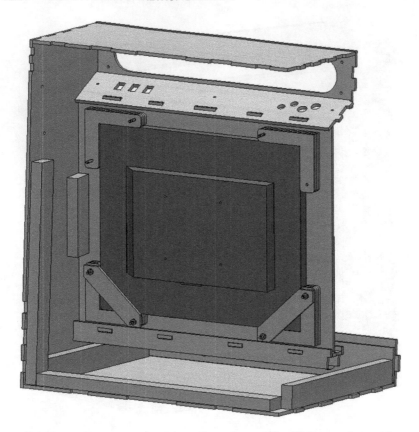

Figure 7-43. *Insert monitor into brackets. You'll know here if you measured wrong :)*

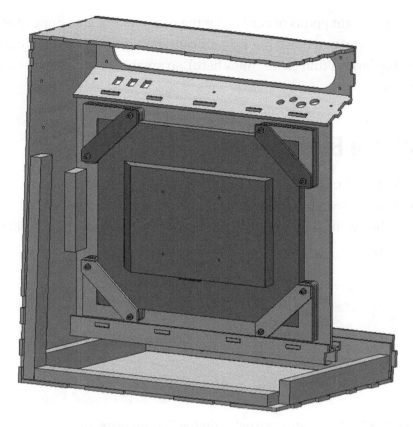

Figure 7-44. *Insert monitor and top cross braces. Fasten with nuts*

Let's recap for a moment. The method just demonstrated here, though lengthy in preparation, is the easiest method to achieve the cleanest looking arcade cabinet LCD installation. It involves a lot of individual measurements and an accurate CAD model (2D or 3D) to convince yourself everything will align, but worth the effort. If you happen to snag a surplus of used PC monitors from a school or business, chances are they are all the same make and model, giving your drawing files extra mileage for other arcade builds. I've tried many other methods to mount LCDs, but this one is tried and true. Not every monitor will be so friendly when broken down to its metal frame. I have found Dell and HP brand monitors are great candidates for arcade building in the methods I've demonstrated. Gateway monitors are not.

We have eight points of contact for the nuts and bolts, so none of these need to be tightened down hard. Significantly snug will do. Remember the acrylic top layer is thin (1/16" thick here), so anything too tight will crack it at the bolt head.

Marquee Button Panel

The hard part is over. With the monitor installed, we can now start populating the switches and electronics. I'll start with the integrated switches below the marquee. Add the various switches and buttons like in Figure 7-45.

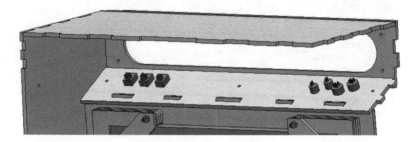

Figure 7-45. *Add buttons and switches below marquee*

Moving to the front view of the arcade in Figure 7-46, add the trim piece to this area (Figure 7-47). I paint this piece separately. Paint it with care as it's somewhat significant as it's a trim piece. This panel is also an accent piece. If you have two or three color scheme this piece can be altered for a color accent.

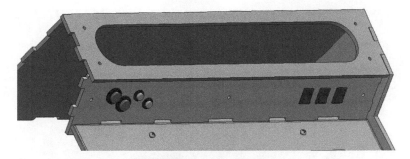

Figure 7-46. *Front view under marquee*

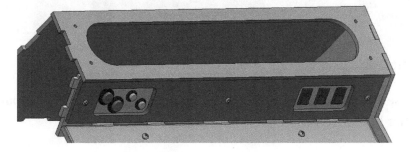

Figure 7-47. *Add trim piece*

This trim piece will mask any poorly painted areas and cover up the cabinet's butt joints and seams which are difficult to paint cleanly.

Control Panel Assembly

The control panel borrows many of the previous techniques in the mini arcade cabinet design. We've double the buttons and the joystick count. These arcade buttons are Suzo-Happ which will help keep the control panel layers fastened together. The Suzo-Happ arcade buttons have a locking nylon nut, great for larger arcades with thicker control panels. I have vector graphics already made for the mini arcade; scaling them up to a larger control panel just takes an hour (Figure 7-48). Alright, it actually took 2 hours. I am no graphic designer.

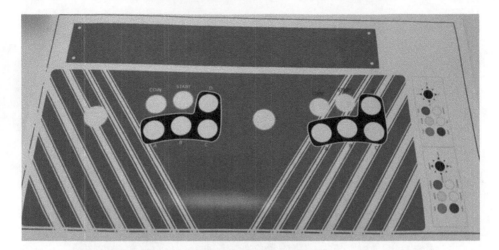

Figure 7-48. *Control panel artwork printed*

Assemble the control panel by gluing the top and bottom wood panels together like in Figure 7-49.

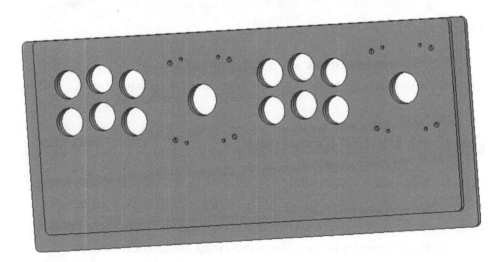

Figure 7-49. *Glue together control panels*

Install both Sanwa JFL joysticks with counter-sunk machine screws, locking split washers, and nuts (Figure 7-50).

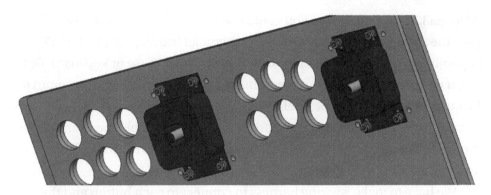

Figure 7-50. *Install joysticks*

Add the artwork and clear acrylic layer on top. The arcade buttons with their locking nuts will keep everything together; refer to Figure 7-51.

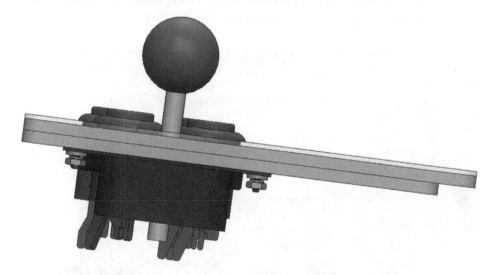

Figure 7-51. *Side view, assembled control panel*

Control Panel Wiring

This control panel necessitates a keyboard emulator (also called a keyboard encoder) based on how many inputs we have to poll. The keyboard emulator I'm using is now discontinued. It was an open source

ATmega32U4-based device. You could use many 32U4 microcontrollers (like the Arduino Micro) as they have one crucial feature, built USB HID capabilities. You can program these to be a custom mouse or keyboard. But if you want something more approachable and lacking having to program it, I would recommend a generic eBay keyboard emulator. However, if you wish to mimic the features of this keyboard encoder- individual reprogrammable inputs, look toward an I-PAC 2 by Ultimarc (`www.ultimarc.com`). I'll talk about individual reprogrammable inputs later.

We have to make a wiring harness to connect to each button and the respective input on the keyboard encoder (preview shown in Figure 7-52). Many eBay keyboard encoders include the wiring harness. This hand wiring is monotonous and time-consuming. If this is your first time wiring a control panel, opt for the solution with prefabricated wiring harnesses. I like to do things the hard way, let's wire this by hand.

Figure 7-52.   *Control panel wiring preview*

To do that, I'll use strips of the wire (about 12 inches) and crimp a quick connect spade connector to each wire end (Figure 7-52).

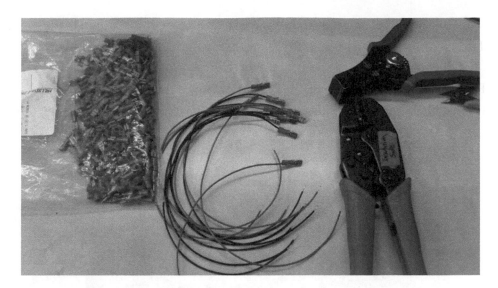

Figure 7-53. *Crimp connectors with wire*

The crimp connects slide into the arcade button microswitch tabs. Referencing Figure 7-54, note we are using the middle tab for the arcade input (action button) and the tab furthest from the button as ground. This is the open circuit loop that is closed when the button is pressed.

Figure 7-54. *Quick connectors on arcade button microswitch*

The Sanwa JFL joystick includes a wiring harness with tinned leads. These connect to their respective directions on the keyboard encoder.

The button below the control panel (front bottom of the arcade in Figure 7-55) is our function (FN) button. Pressing this button will double the usable buttons mapping assignments—sort of like a "shift" key.

Figure 7-55. *The "function" button*

This shift key will aide with EmulationStation navigation and other high-level controls like exiting a ROM or toggling a configuration menu (F1). It helps tremendously to write down what the game controls should be along with the shifted functions. We want to avoid duplicate key assignments and any hotkeys used by default in RetroArch. For example, video filters are assigned to keys "M" and "N" in RetroArch, so I actively avoid those keys. Figure 7-56 demonstrates one configuration.

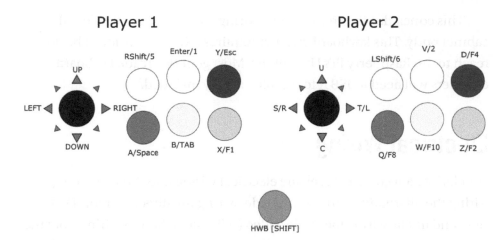

Figure 7-56. *A suggested two-player key mapping configuration*

The first key mapping (denoted as xx in the xx/yy placeholder labeling) is the normal state triggered during game play. The second key mapping (yy) is the shifted function. The lower front panel button must be held down to use the alternate key assignment. With a written diagram to follow, I used the supplied programmer to make these key assignments (Figure 7-57).

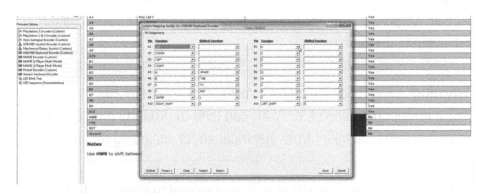

Figure 7-57. *Programming keyboard key mappings*

This concludes the control panel wiring. You can place this into the cabinet body. This keyboard encoder requires a USB extension cable to reach to the Raspberry Pi's USB inputs. Most generic arcade keyboard encoders will need a USB A to B cable, usually included.

Electrical Wiring

For clarity I am going to break the electrical wiring into three main steps: wiring the alternating current (AC) side, wiring the direct current (DC) side, and finally wiring the audio/video (A/V) side. I'll start wiring from the source, getting power from your wall outlet and distributing that into the arcade cabinet.

AC Wiring

We are building a larger cabinet; therefore, we need more power. The easiest way to supply more power is to land a more versatile power source into the cabinet, this being 120V AC. This is general appliance power. Your toaster uses this power. Your TV uses this power. We are simply going to place an AC power strip into the arcade cabinet, but with some custom and cheaper alternatives.

Warning   The following steps involve working with 120V AC. Improper handling of 120V AC can lead to property damage like fires and personal injury from electrical shock including death.

Figure 7-58 shows the wiring harness we need to fabricate. It is comprised of (from lower left to right) an IEC appliance cord cut short to the female end, a single gang outlet, a double-pole-single throw AC switch, and an IEC appliance female socket. Any exposed AC connection points are isolated from stray hands and fingers by using a mix of new and old-work electrical boxes (pictured blue if you have a colored version of this book). Again, this is nothing more than a glorified AC power strip, and one can take the place of this. Our goal here is to build an arcade for the user, so a clean, thoughtful integration of power is our goal here.

Figure 7-58. *AC wiring harness*

Figures 7-59 through 7-61 show detailed close-ups of some of the components needed to create this harness. In order, these are IEC 60320 appliance cable (we need one to chop for this harness and one for the arcade), single gang outlet, and a IEC female socket (Figure 7-61 left) and a panel mount two-pole double-throw AC switch (Figure 7-61 right).

Figure 7-59. *IEC appliance cord*

Figure 7-60. *Single gang electrical outlet with cover*

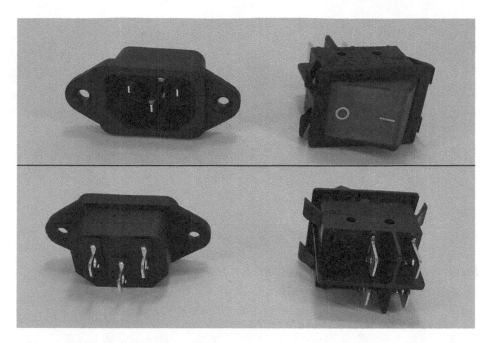

Figure 7-61. *IEC female socket (left) and two-pole double throw AC panel mount switch (right)*

You will need a quality pair of wire strippers for this job. Wire strippers/pliers with a crimp section are also very handy here like in Figure 7-62 left. If you plan to do this often, I suggest a dedicated wire stripper and crimp tool (middle and right items in Figure 7-62). Figure 7-63 shows a few types of crimp connectors used in this arcade build.

Note   All the crimp connectors used in this book are for 22-16 AWG (American wire gauge). This is the red-colored insulation jack end for those who are reading in the black and white.

A sharp utility knife (not pictured) is also needed to cut away the thick jacket insulation of the appliance cord.

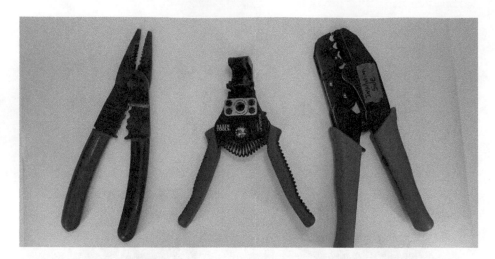

Figure 7-62. *Electrical tools from left to right; wire strippers, auto wire strippers, and crimp tool*

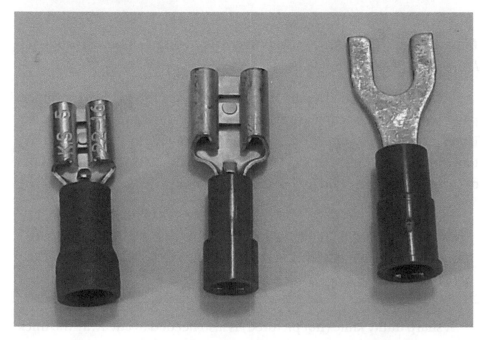

Figure 7-63. *Crimp connectors from left to right: 0.187 inch female, 0.25 inch female, and spade connector*

Before we start wiring, let's look at a diagram of our harness in Figure 7-64.

Figure 7-64. *Diagram of AC wiring harness*

Removing the cover plates and electrical boxes (Figure 7-65) illustrates how to wire this harness. Stripping away the appliance cable insulation should reveal three conductors likely colored: black, white, and green. In the United States, the hot wire is black, the neutral wire is white, and green is ground.

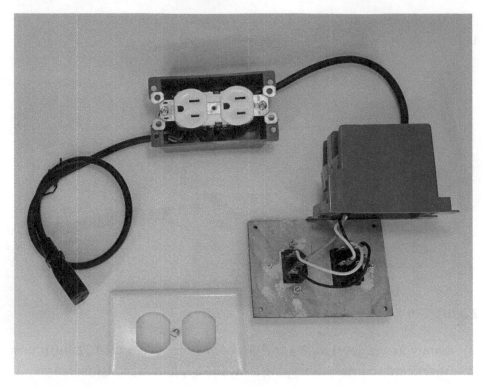

Figure 7-65. *AC wiring harness with cover plates removed*

Figures 7-66 through 7-69 provide the wiring diagrams.

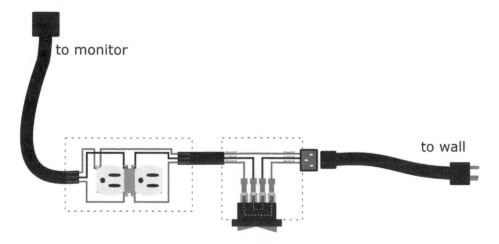

Figure 7-66. *AC harness wiring diagram, overview*

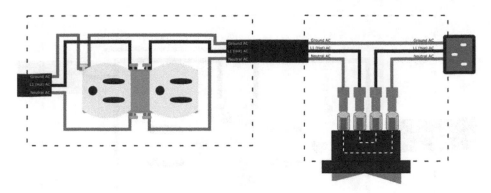

Figure 7-67. *AC harness wiring diagram close-up*

Figures 7-68 and 7-69 are larger diagrams of the switch + IEC socket and single gang outlet, respectively.

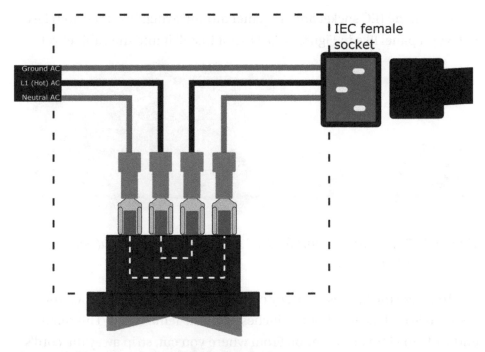

Figure 7-68. *Close of switch + IEC socket*

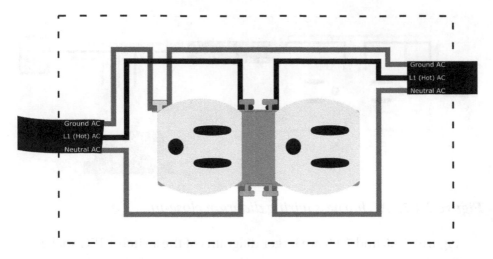

Figure 7-69. *Close-up of outlet wiring*

Mount the IEC socket and AC panel mount switch in our custom laser cut wood panel like in Figure 7-70. Do not install it into the cabinet yet.

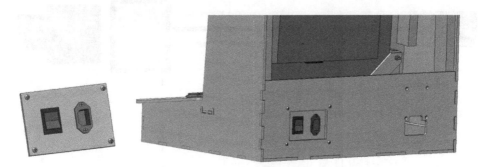

Figure 7-70. *Wood mount for IEC socket and AC switch(left), installed into cabinet (right)*

To create the harness, start by cutting the IEC appliance cable from the female end. Leave about 18 inches from the female end. This female end will plug into our monitor. From where you cut, strip away the cord's insulation and expose the hot, neutral, and ground conductors. Strip some insulation from the conductors and crimp the appropriate terminals to the ends and wire the outlet in parallel. From the outlet, cut a short section of cable from the unused male end of the appliance cable. Wire each leg (hot and neutral) into the switch. Ground gets passed through directly to the IEC outlet. With your leftover cable length, strip off some conductors to wire the other side of the switch (hot and neutral) to the IEC outlet. See Figures 7-71 and 7-72 for close-ups of connections to the IEC socket, switch, and outlet.

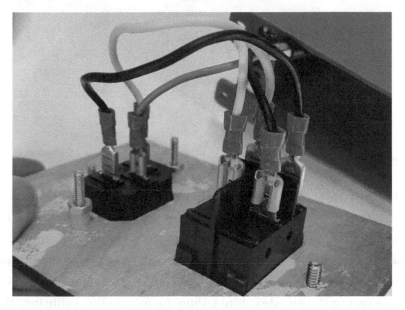

Figure 7-71. *AC harness close-up IEC socket and panel mount double-pole single-throw switch*

Figure 7-72. *AC harness close-up outlet*

Our custom faceplate with the switch and IEC female socket gets mounted to a deep electrical box. Like the outlet, this covers exposed conductors. This is generally a smart practice while working with AC and the idea your hands/arms will be anywhere near it, accidentally or intentionally. Mount the IEC socket and AC switch faceplate assembly inside the rear or the arcade cabinet. Plug the female IEC cable into the monitor's power input.

Remember, this is 120VAC. If you're in Europe and following along, then you're around 240 volts AC. Either way, mistakes in this harness could at minimum create a short circuit and trip a breaker. Worst-case scenario, you could start an electrical fire or electrocute yourself, causing serious bodily harm or even death. Be absolutely sure your wiring is correct. Do not do this unless you are a trained electrician. If you are a trained electrician, please do not tell OSHA about this section.

DC Wiring

I'll be honest with you, I made this arcade about a year ago and the inside looked like in Figure 7-73. You have to understand, I've always heeded the advice, if you don't want anyone to see the poor job you did, simply hide your work in a box. Since I've been writing this book, I didn't want to immortalize myself with that reputation. So I've cleaned up my act in Figure 7-74.

Figure 7-73. *Everything wired, before I knew I'd be writing a book*

Figure 7-74. *Everything rewired, after I knew I was writing a book*

Either way, there are a few methods to wire the DC portion of this arcade. Less is at stake here (as in hazards to our self), so one could simply "get the job done" or redo the entire job knowing you have to take photos that will eventually be seen in print.

If you're of the method, just get it done, great! We are of the same mindset. You'll need one extra component to do the sloppy method; a barrier strip like in Figure 7-75 (and featured in Figure 7-73). The barrier strip is just a distribution bus of screw terminals.

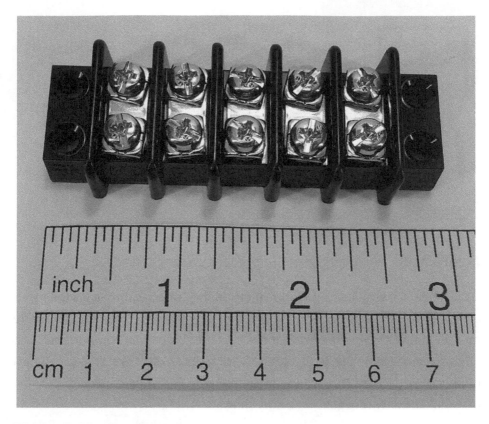

Figure 7-75. *Barrier strip*

It makes for quick work, but as I retraced my old wiring to clean up this cabinet and integrate my power block PCB, organization can get away from you easily when using a barrier stip. With an abundances of locations to land power and ground connections, it makes for quick and dirty work than a thoughtful layout. "But who's gonna see it anyway?"

Alright, enough of endorsing bad habits. I've updated our wiring diagram to show the DC side of things in Figure 7-76.

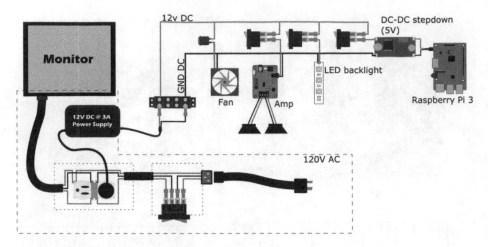

Figure 7-76. *Wiring diagram with DC section*

The barrier strip just shows one method to wire this cabinet. It's the most approachable method and even allows for later changes/expansion for future modifications. This cabinet has a focus to power individual components in a downstream fashion like in Figure 7-77. Sometimes, electrical wiring can be a difficult task because it's hard to envision. Figure 7-77 represents another way to visualize our wiring goals as a flow chart.

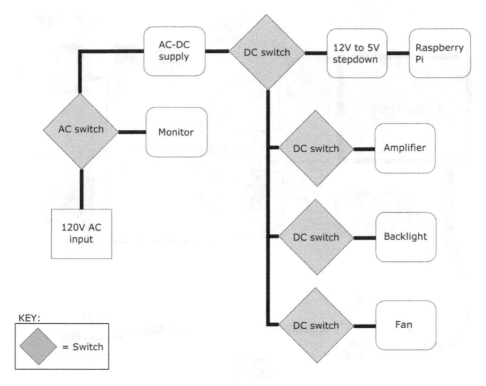

Figure 7-77. *DC wiring diagram written as a flow chart*

But why this configuration you ask? I don't know. I like the feeling of flipping lots of switches to turn something on. A better explanation is for flexibility and expandability. In the future, what if you want a different PC connected to the VGA input of the monitor? We need way to power off the Raspberry Pi when it's not in use. What if you want to mute the speakers? I actually have this arcade next to my TV in my living room. It's a great second screen, but there's no need to have speakers on when the main TV is in use. Lastly, the backlight is just for show—it does not need to be on all the time.

If you're using a custom PCB to do most of the switch and power distribution (like the Power Block Arcade PCB seen in the previous chapter), then the overall wiring will look like Figure 7-78. Configuration is the same as Figures 7-76 and 7-77.

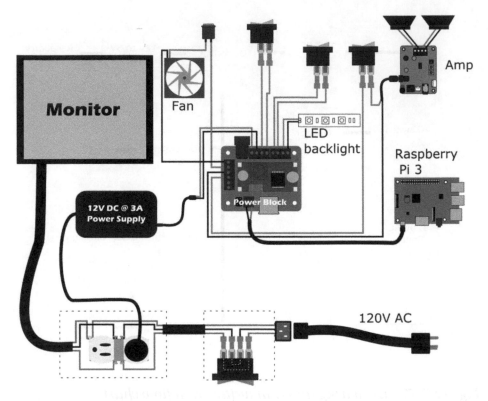

Figure 7-78. *DC wiring with Arcade Power Block*

In either wiring method, the 12VDC supply is just a wall adapter, the same used to power the entire mini arcade. The difference here is this 12V DC power supply is now housed on the inside of this larger arcade cabinet suppling power to everything except the monitor.

Audio and Video Wiring

The last electrical task to do here is connect any remaining audio and video cables like in Figure 7-79. This monitor uses DVI input, so we need a HDMI to DVI cable to connect between the Raspberry Pi and the monitor. Audio will have to remain as analog, and to avoid any ground loop issues within our audio signal, I recommend a ground loop isolator.

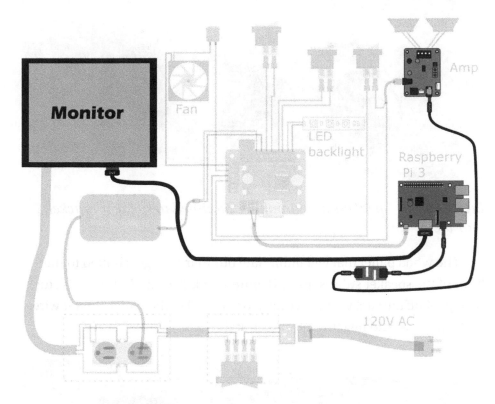

Figure 7-79. *Audio and video wiring*

Speaking of audio, we need to mount our speakers and amp inside the arcade. No new techniques here. Just bigger speakers and a larger bracket to mount as shown in Figure 7-80.

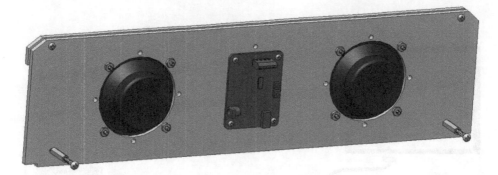

Figure 7-80. *Speakers and amplifier mounted to speaker bracket, rear view*

The wood panel that will illuminate our marquee gets bolted to the front of the speaker subassembly (Figure 7-81). The 12V LED strip is stuck (just peel off the sticky adhesive back protector) to the panel. Solder wires to the positive and negative terminals at the end.

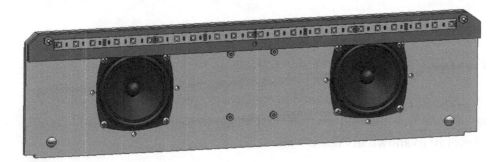

Figure 7-81. *LEDs, speakers, and amplifier mounted to speaker bracket, front view*

Add the brackets for the left and right sides of the cabinet and secure with nuts and bolts as shown in Figure 7-82.

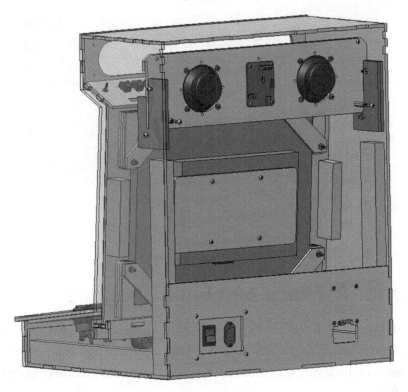

Figure 7-82. *Speaker brackets and speaker subassembly installed in cabinet*

While we are here, let's mount the Raspberry Pi into the rear panel (see Figure 7-83).

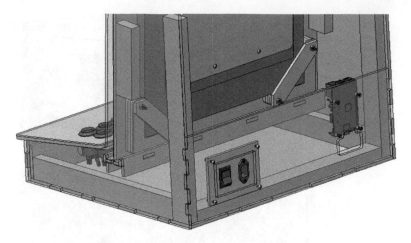

Figure 7-83. *Mount Raspberry Pi*

Exterior Artwork and Final Touches

We still have some finishing touches to apply to the arcade like the vinyl artwork and the marquee artwork. Place the marquee artwork between two clear acrylic layers and mount into the front of the arcade (Figures 7-84 and 7-85).

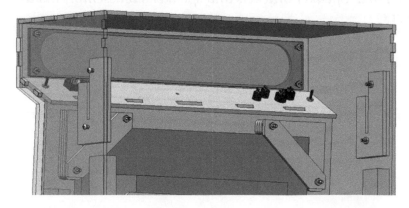

Figure 7-84. *Acrylic marquee layers*

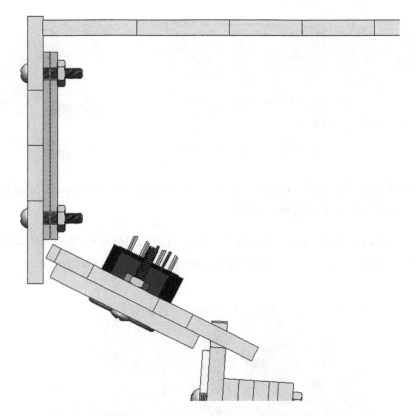

Figure 7-85. *Artwork is placed between acrylic layers*

Because the acrylic is so thin (each panel is about 1/16th inch thick), the span is so long it is possible the acrylic panels might sag in the middle and consequently pull away from the front of the marquee. To prevent this, I cut a small slotted square. It is mounted inside (Figure 7-86) with a nut and bolt. This slotted rectangle pushes up against the acrylic panels, keeping them flush with the face of the marquee.

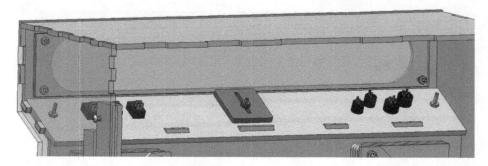

Figure 7-86. *Slotted rectangle to push against acrylic layers and keep them flush again marquee front*

If you haven't already, plug the keyboard encoder into the USB slot of the Raspberry Pi and insert a RetroPie-loaded SD card (Figure 7-87).

Figure 7-87. *Connect keyboard encoder (USB) and insert SD card with RetroPie image*

Optional but recommended for extended play, mount a PC fan to the rear panel. Our monitor is from an older era, so it does emit some heat. Keeping it cool will extend its life and that's in our best interest. This is a custom-mounted LCD panel in a custom arcade cabinet, best to give the monitor the longest life possible by keeping it cool and the cabinet actively ventilated.

The rear panel also has a spare tab glued from the inside at the bottom. This locks the bottom of the panel and keeps it flush with the lower rear I/O panel. Totally optional, but if the rear panel warps or bows just slightly from all the paint, this may alleviate the warping. I had some warping. See if you can spot the troublesome area by comparing the bottom and top seams of the rear panel in Figure 7-88.

Figure 7-88. *Fan installed on rear panel. Fan grill (finger guard) is attached on opposite side*

Finally, add the rear panel to the cabinet and fasten with screws. Plug the IEC appliance cable into the rear of the cabinet (Figure 7-89). The rear panel attaches to the speaker subassembly with female-female threaded standoffs (Figure 7-90).

Figure 7-89. *Mount rear panel and plug in*

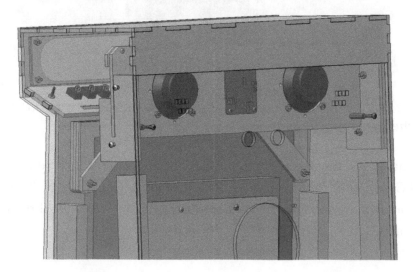

Figure 7-90. *Fasten rear panel to speaker bracket with female-female standoffs*

Well done! You've just completed (or watched me complete) a desktop arcade for two players.

Cost Breakdown and Bill of Materials

I saved this section last because it's very subjective. The cost of building an arcade can be pricey, especially if this is your first build. A "cold start" might involve buying the majority of the supplies and tools you need to actually build the arcade cabinet. A few hundred dollars in hand and power tools make the startup cost high. Add on the rest of the electronic components and many people are turned off by the initial cost. I understand completely. This arcade build focuses on being resourceful. We reused a free PC monitor from the late 2000s, salvaged a PC fan from a dead computer power supply. Your mileage will vary. I have access to a number of specialty tools (laser cutters, general wood working equipment, 24 inch-wide inkjet printers) and have been building arcades for a few years. Most of the startup costs to build an arcade I've already recuperated. Seeing returns on using my tools frequently or buying in bulk and reselling can offset costs too. *Remember, the savings you get from buying in bulk is only recouped if you're using or reselling the bulk items.* Selling your work will also recuperate the costs of your supplies and tools. The more you sell (economies of scale), the more costs you can offset to fund your hobby. Build one arcade for yourself, build two more to sell (always keep the nicer one).

So what did this arcade cost? My cost is just under $210. Table 7-1 shows my expenses to build the arcade featured in this chapter.

Table 7-1. *Ryan's cost breakdown*

Qty	Description	Vendor	Cost	Line Cost
1	Wood: 1/4" underlayment plywood	Lowes	$13.50	$13.50
1.5	Acrylic 1/16" x 24x18" sheet		$9.00	$13.50
1	Laser cutting		$0.00	$0.00
1	Paint, oil-based primer	Hardware store	$2.00	$2.00
1	Spray paint, cherry red	Hardware store	$4.95	$4.95
1	Paint brush, foam	Hardware store	$0.75	$0.75
3	Sandpaper, disks 400, 220 100	Harbor Freight	$0.50	$1.50
1	Photo paper; Artwork for Control Panel and marquee, 24in wide		$6.00	$6.00
13	Happ arcade buttons	na.suzohapp.com	$1.45	$18.85
2	Sanwa joystick, JFL-TP-8Y	eBay.com	$15.00	$30.00
2	Button w/ LED 16mm	eBay.com	$0.50	$1.00
3	Switch SPST rocker	eBay.com	$0.50	$1.50
2	Switch, round 12mm	eBay.com	$0.40	$0.80
1	IEC female socket	Parts-Express.com	$1.95	$1.95
1	Switch, rocker DPST AC	eBay.com	$3.50	$3.50
1	IEC receptacle 15A/125v	Parts-Express.com	$1.36	$1.36
1	Single gang PVC shallow electrical box	Hardware store	$0.98	$0.98
1	Single gang PVC old work electrical box	Hardware store	$1.01	$1.01

(continued)

Table 7-1. (*continued*)

Qty	Description	Vendor	Cost	Line Cost
49	Quick connect crimp	Parts-Express.com	$0.07	$3.43
2	IEC appliance (power) cable	thrift store	$0.00	$0.00
1	Monitor 17" Dell	yard sale	$0.00	$0.00
1	HDMI to DVI cable, 3ft	eBay.com	$3.00	$3.00
1	Stereo audio cable, 3ft	eBay.com	$1.00	$1.00
1	Raspberry Pi 3	newark.com	$35.00	$35.00
1	SD card, 8GB class 10 SanDisk	amazon.com	$8.00	$8.00
1	DC-DC step-down converter	eBay.com	$2.00	$2.00
10	Wires 22 AWG 1ft		$0.50	$5.00
2	Speakers	Parts-Express.com	$3.50	$7.00
1	Amplifier, 2 Watt, stereo	Parts-Express.com	$8.00	$8.00
1	Keyboard encoder	eBay.com	$10.00	$10.00
3	Vinyl, white, 1 Sq ft		$3.00	$9.00
1	Vinyl cutting Labor 1Hr		$0.00	$0.00
1	Poster board, black	dollar store	$1.00	$1.00
97	#8-32, 6-32, 4-40 nuts + bolts	mcmaster.com	$0.05	$4.85
1	12V 2A power supply	eBay.com	$8.00	$8.00
14	Labor (hours)		$0.00	$0.00
		TOTAL		**$208.43**

A few things to note, my labor cost is marked as $0/per hour because this is a "fun" hobby and these arcades are for the home. Realistically, that might not work in a true accounting setting. This is the same for laser cutting; I do the laser cutting. If you want to do this professionally, well that labor cost number won't be zero. Other small details like a quart of white primer is something like $12 for a decent brand, but I only have $2 marked. This quart of paint will cover at least six arcades, so that divided cost is factored in this total cost. I purchase speaker amplifiers, arcade buttons, joysticks, and nuts and bolt hardware in bulk. This gets me vendor pricing or bulk pricing. This saves about 20–30% of the list price.

What is a typical cost for first time builder? About $335. In this scenario, you're outsourcing some of the heavy lifting like laser cutting and using a print shop to print your graphic artwork. You're also buying for one cabinet, so without bulk discounts, most individual component costs are marked up by 20%. This build still counts on finding a monitor for free. If not, expect to increase this total by another $40 to $100 (depends on the monitor that fits your needs). If buying a new monitor, a reasonable range to build this arcade is between $370 and $450.

For the experienced builder (and not including the CAD design), total assembly time is about 14 hours (this doesn't include paint drying). An arcade like this will likely take two weekends, or about four consecutive days with proper planning and ignoring hiccups like inclement weather if you paint outside.

As a last topic to consider is your labor cost. It's never truly "free." Once you become proficient in cabinet building, consider your labor cost. Building and designing from scratch encompasses disciplines like graphic design, electrical engineering technology, IT and computer science, CAD, and mechanical engineering. This is skilled labor and should be accounted for.

Summary

You might not have the skills to build the perfect arcade on your first try, but hopefully you will enjoy the time spent honing current skills while learning new ones. I hope I've shown you it can be done. Where do you start? Anywhere! Just start. You can always build another arcade. The next one is always just a little bit better than the previous and if it's made by your hands, you love it unconditionally.

Index

© Mark Frauenfelder and Ryan Bates 2019
M. Frauenfelder and R. Bates, *Raspberry Pi Retro Gaming*,
https://doi.org/10.1007/978-1-4842-5153-9